Room at My Table

What I loved about *Room at My Table* was that you could smell the food, feel the welcome and wish that you could be part of the delightful conversations. Evelyn Bence writes about hospitality out of the real life events where she has opened her home to friends, to the neighbors, and to that inevitable child who somehow appears in all of our lives, just waiting to be invited in. This is definitely a keeper, taking a place along with all the other volumes on the shelf that expand my understanding of this well-loved topic—hospitality.

—Karen Mains, director, Hungry Souls,
author of *Open Heart, Open Home*

Evelyn . . . invited me to think through the spiritual implications of a life of hospitality and what it could look like. I encourage you to take her up on the same invitation. As you read *Room at My Table*, I'm guessing God just might touch your heart too.

—Anita Lustrea, radio talk show host, speaker,
and author of *Shades of Mercy* and *What Women Tell Me*

I have eaten at Evelyn's table. What she has written is also what she has lived. Most of us make our major life decisions with others around food. Jesus did the same. This is a "one of a kind" devotional . . . compelling . . . captures Jesus' life and invites us to discover this richness of life.

—Jo Anne Lyon, general superintendent of The Wesleyan Church
and author of *The Ultimate Blessing*

For those who want to embrace people in hospitality but don't think they can; for those who *don't* want to but think they should—this is the book to read! Read it slowly (if you can!) or read it quickly (as did I) then go back and integrate these inspiring thoughts into your own life. *Room at My Table* will make it onto the short list of books that occupy my limited bookshelves. And it is already on my gift list for special people and occasions!

—Miriam Huffman Rockness, author of *Home: God's Design*
and *Passion for the Impossible*

Evelyn Bence weaves together the practical and the spiritual, the moments of friendship in her living room, and the mystery of God's welcome to us. Bence's insights and questions call us to reflect more deeply both on how we serve our friends and how we respond to Christ who has invited us to his table. A delectable collection of meditations.

—Kristina LaCelle-Peterson, author of *Liberating Tradition*
and associate professor of religion at Houghton College

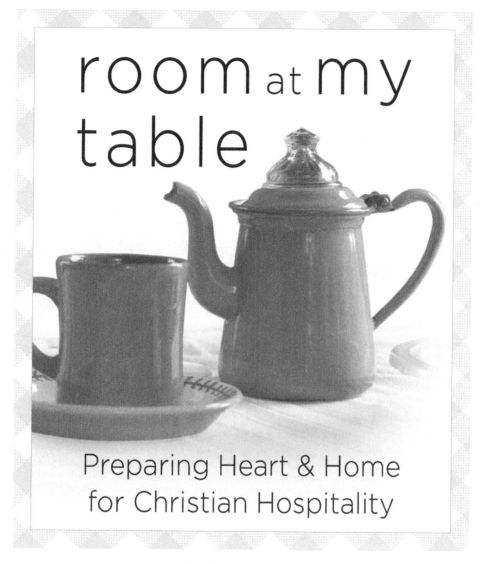

room at my table

Preparing Heart & Home
for Christian Hospitality

Evelyn
Bence

UPPER
ROOM BOOKS®
NASHVILLE

LIBRARY OF CONGRESS CATALOGING-IN-PUBLICATION DATA

Bence, Evelyn.
  Room at my table : preparing heart and home for Christian hospitality /
Evelyn Bence.
    pages cm
  ISBN 978-0-8358-1359-4 (print)—ISBN 978-0-8358-1360-0 (mobi)—ISBN
978-0-8358-1361-7 (epub)
  1. Hospitality—Religious aspects—Christianity. 2. Dinners and
dining—Religious aspects—Christianity. I. Title.
  BV4647.H67B37 2014
  241'.4—dc23
                              2013049099

Printed in the United States of America

To my dad—with gregariousness and generosity,
   he invited friends and strangers to the table.
To my mother—with resourcefulness and graciousness,
   she made do and made room.
Together, they modeled hospitality and forged memories
   that have molded this book.

Thank you—
To guests who have graced my home now and again over
   decades: no guests, no stories about hosting.
To Camilla, whose friendship and hospitality increased my
   culinary knowledge, my hosting wisdom, and my favor as a
   guest.
To the Upper Room team: Jeannie Crawford-Lee, who responded
   enthusiastically to sample chapters; John Mogabgab, who
   shepherded me through the hoops; and Janice Neely, who
   connected me to new markets.
To my readers: the hope of your picking up this book has kept
   me writing.

Contents

Part 3   Serving Up Soup

Part 4   Sitting at Table

Part 5   Savoring the Taste

Introduction

It is striking how much of Jesus' life is told in settings defined by meals.
—EUGENE PETERSON

Hospitality. Though the word's cordial welcome encompasses more than culinary service, this book focuses on the host's role of feeding people, particularly those outside the immediate family circle, with its attendant obligations.

Hospitality has been characterized as a gift, even a spiritual gift, though it is not listed as such in the New Testament. There's no mistaking that some people have natural abilities in the kitchen, in the organizational sphere, in the conversational corner. That's why it's so tempting to avoid responsibility: hospitality, it's not my gift.

But the Bible calls for everyone to give it a try: "Contribute to the needs of the saints and seek to show hospitality," writes Paul (Rom. 12:13). Other epistle writers add qualifying phrases: "Show hospitality to one another without grumbling" (1 Pet. 4:9). And "Do not neglect to show hospitality to strangers" (Heb. 13:2).

You may be a high-profile hostess with a sixty-inch range. I'm not, never have been. I have a bare-bones galley kitchen, not even a dishwasher. I have people over. I make it work.

Maybe your kitchen isn't your handicap, but it's easy for you to name another: your spouse or children, your workload, limited parking, insufficient seating. Most anyone can find a reason for not reaching out . . .

But these fifty-two meditations are not about *should*. They don't present a theology or a scriptural study of biblical hospitality. Nor would you find them in *Better Homes and Gardens*. Drawing on my own experiences—the successes as well as the failures—I've gone for encouragement. Dip in. Here's what I hope you'll find:

For hosts known for their hospitable grace and discerning culinary taste, if not skill—encouragement, camaraderie, invigoration.

For fledglings curious or envious of others who exhibit hospitable grace and culinary skill—in story form, an inspirational primer for taking a first step toward a personal success.

For guests anticipating or grateful for hospitable grace and culinary taste and sneaking a preview—a nicely packaged gift.

For nostalgics pining for the good old days when people knew something about hospitality and grace—a smidge of humor and a handful of hope that the art hasn't been lost, as some claim.

For people hungry for relationships grounded in real time—an invitation to reach out and enjoy face-to-face connections: table talk.

If you read these pieces straight through, you might think that I welcome guests every weekend, which is hardly the case. This material is a condensation of decades' worth of hospitable culinary opportunities, presented with some names changed and a few details disguised.

"Come and eat. Here, drink something." The invitation never loses its potential: a parent speaking to a toddler, a friend suggesting lunch, a neighbor coaxing a grieving widow, a colleague hosting a barbecue or buffet. The invitation's appeal is rooted deep in our humanity; we are, after all, newly needy—hungry and thirsty—every day. And in our tradition: King David welcoming Saul's grandson to his table like one of his own; Jesus cooking breakfast for his disciples; and the writer of the last biblical chapter beckoning the thirsty to come to the water of life.

Some contemporary invitations are vicarious and virtual, broadcast by smiling chefs talking to cameras in studios. But the best invitations are real and sincere: I'd be honored for you to sit at my table.

Here and now, I'd be honored for you to turn the page and read a prelude, introducing the meditations from my heart and a few recipes served at my table.

Prelude: Water with Ice, Please

A woman from Samaria came to draw water. Jesus said to her, "Give me a drink."... Jesus answered her, "If you knew the gift of God, and who it is that is saying to you, 'Give me a drink,' you would have asked him, and he would have given you living water."

—JOHN 4:7, 10

If God is willing to use something as basic as water to get our attention, what else might he use?

—MARGARET FEINBERG

N one?" Had I possibly misunderstood the church sexton? At coffee hour I'd noticed a need—empty lemonade pitchers—and requested replenishment.

"Yes, but we have no ice," Willem explained. Nor had there been any the previous Sunday. No ten-pound bag, often melded into a solid block. No cube trays, full or empty. And this on a hundred-degree day when the air conditioner wasn't holding its own.

"What? Why?"

"The church no longer offers ice. And the ice cube trays were given to the Salvation Army." Surely there'd been a breakdown of communication.

Hot and very bothered, I immediately drove to the nearest convenience store and returned to the church hugging a big bag of ice. Did my consider-the-many-benefits-of-ice memo to the pastor stem the warm tide of change? I don't know. The church kitchen did soon reinstate its offering of ice.

When serving dinner guests, I've repeatedly noticed that I can run out of iced tea, hot coffee, soda, or fruit-based beverage . . . and no one seems to mind . . . if I point out the pitcher of ice water set near the middle of the table or, better yet, like a steward top off everyone's glass. Nothing fancy. Just "cool, clear water," to quote Bob Nolan, the song-writer behind the Johnny Cash classic.

Jesus himself, who knew something about fine wine, commended the person who gives "even a cup of cold water" (Matt. 10:42)—a service I've provided daily for more than a year.

It's such a basic, raw request that it tears at my heart. Virtually every day a neighbor girl who comes by to read books and sing songs asks for "water with ice." She sometimes whispers the words, as if it's our secret. She usually adds "please." When prompted I reach for a specific mug, decorated with angels, and fill it with tap water and, count them, four cubes of ice.

One Sunday morning as I handed her the cold mug, I looked straight into her intense brown eyes and saw her thirst for sustenance supplied with personal attention. "It's like Jesus giving you water." I hadn't intended to say it out loud, but the keen ears behind the big eyes . . . she heard me.

Her grip firmly grasping cool emblazed angels, she smiled and whispered, "Yes it is."

God, sometimes circumstances seem to require a feast.
But if all you ask us to provide is chilled water, bless our gifts.
Bless us as we give. Bless those who receive.

part 1

Setting the Scene

*Even an innate inclination to hospitality must
be honed and refined, imbued and filled if it is
to be more than concern about centerpieces,
menus, table settings, and spotless rooms.*
—KAREN MAINS

The Pressure of Perfect

If possible, so far as it depends on you, live peaceably with all.
—ROMANS 12:18

Several of my sisters and I were discussing basic plans for an upcoming family reunion—not encompassing a many-branched family tree but only our parents' descendants. We had previously set a date and chosen a central county in which to gather. But now, with deadlines approaching, even the few of us, not a quorum, had differing preferences and priorities for ourselves, our children, and our grandchildren. Should we work with a caterer or buy deli salads and watermelon? Should we grill meat? Should we rent a church hall (air-conditioned and rainproof but confining) or reserve a pavilion in a lakeside park (swimming opportunities, weather permitting)?

We fussed over the immediate decision: indoors or outdoors? The informally agreed-upon point person finally articulated the underlying problem: "I don't want to take the responsibility." *I don't want to be blamed if people are disappointed.*

Intentionally trying to release the pressure, I started repeating a phrase: "It's not going to be a perfect day." *We won't please everyone—across three generations. We can't—mustn't—put that burden on ourselves.* My sisters got tired of my watchword, but the message got through.

We're going with the outdoor venue, catering to the children more than the grandparents. We're grilling burgers and buying deli sides. I sense that we're all anticipating the event, even the unofficial hostess.

Romans 12 includes a substantial listing of godly *shoulds*. Most of them, including "[Be] given to hospitality" (v. 13, KJV), concern community life. In the middle of the exhortations the apostle interjects a caveat, which the poetic King James renders "If it be possible, as much as lieth in you . . ." (Rom. 12:18).

Planning a perfect event that will delight everyone—introvert, extrovert, athlete, bookworm, diabetic, vegan, old curmudgeon, young prima donna—is not a reasonable goal. If it be possible . . . make every effort . . . act in good faith . . . anticipate the gathering.

By the way: On our reunion day it rained. But we later realized that the inclement weather made the day nearly perfect. We enjoyed a lakeside view and fresh air, but the drizzle kept us under the pavilion rather than scattered around the park. The highlights of the day were intergenerational conversations: small groups, formed fluidly around nachos, coleslaw, and watermelon.

God, remind me that my best efforts will not please all my guests. Grace my role as hostess with reasonable expectations—my own as well as others'.

making it yours

1. What does "perfect" mean for you? For a real or hypothetical future gathering, quickly jot down some elements that would contribute to a Goldilocks pronouncement of "just right." What, if any, of those elements are beyond your control (e.g., weather, seating constraints)?

2. What might a "good enough" reasonable effort look like?

3. Write your own prayer conversation with God about what "as much as lieth in you" might mean.

Redding Up the House

Precisely because human beings are both physical
and spiritual beings, even so profoundly physical a discipline
as housekeeping has a spiritual dimension.
—MARGARET KIM PETERSON

Let's just say my house was untidy the morning I turned the radio dial to a station celebrating "Christmas in July." It being off-season, I paid special attention to the lineup. By late afternoon they'd played one carol four times: "Joy to the World." Each time I heard one line as if it were a command: "Let every heart prepare him room." By evening I was puzzled: *Lord, what does that mean? How do I "prepare you room"?*

That evening I rather impulsively invited friends over for dinner on the following Saturday night. Suddenly, redding up the house became a priority. I emptied wastebaskets and discarded clutter. I put away valued items I had carelessly left lying around. I vacuumed, wiped, and washed. I even rubbed a shine onto neglected silver-plated iced-tea spoons. Finally I brought in fresh groceries, which I served on a table set with extra plates, surrounded by extra chairs. When Pat and Dawn and the others knocked on the door, I was ready with a hearty welcome.

In preparing for visitors, I identified actions I'm now incorporating into my spiritual life: Discarding the unsightly. Valuing the good. Cleaning the dirty. Tending the true. Bringing in the fresh. Making room for a guest.

Lord, you are the unseen guest at every meal. Give me grace and strength to prepare myself and my home to welcome you.

making it yours

1. Consider the six preparations identified in the last paragraph of the meditation. List or number them, prioritizing the housekeeping needs currently evident in your living room, kitchen, or dining area.

2. Choose one preparatory housekeeping chore to complete today, possibly something that will dramatically improve your environment. The better look can encourage you to take on a second task.

3. Prayerfully prioritize similar metaphorical elements of your spiritual housekeeping. Listening to the Spirit of Christ, choose one or more ways to "prepare him room" in your spiritual home.

Have I Got a Plan for You!

Love must be sincere.
—ROMANS 12:9, NIV

Be kindly affectioned one to another with brotherly love;
in honour preferring one another.
—ROMANS 12:10, KJV

I had a great idea. I would host a Saturday birthday expedition for my friend Meg, born in late March. I'd pack a breakfast for five—the party including her husband and mutual friends. We'd beat the crowds at Washington's Tidal Basin along the Potomac and enjoy a 6:30 picnic among the famed cherry trees, blossoming early that year. Who wouldn't want to?

I can very quickly jump to the end of this story. The picnic never materialized. Have I mentioned that Meg lived in the outer suburbs? My plan required her driving twenty miles one way, rising way before dawn, bundling against the morning chill, sitting on a quilt on the ground—not at a table . . .

Meg considered the proposal and then called back to thank me for my thoughtfulness. "But that's just not what I want to do on my birthday."

I inhaled silently. The conversation ended awkwardly. Neither of us proposed an alternate get-together. I could only assume she celebrated well.

For days I nursed my wounded pride. On Saturday I slept in, having lost any compelling drive to go downtown and breathe the pollen.

Now, twenty years later, Meg and I can laugh about this ill-fated invitation. But I've never again been so bold as to lay out a specific plan—this is it; can you be there?—to honor a friend. Maybe my hesitance indicates my lack of confidence. Maybe it is a sign of maturity—not presuming that my preferred setting would provide the be-all fête. Though I may sometimes wish it were so, the party is not all about me.

God, I rather like the age-old biblical phrasing "in honour preferring one another." As I plan any future gatherings, bring this line to mind.

making it yours

1. Think of someone you'd like to honor. Consider how you'd go about planning a gathering that would suit that person's personality but also be doable for you. (A little "stretch" can energize a hostess. But skydiving, maybe not.) Take into account your schedule, budget, resources, and available settings.

2. Just for fun, imagine what you'd like to do on your next birthday. Consider ways to commemorate "your day" by preferentially reaching out to others.

3. Compose a prayer that, if published, might be titled "The Party Is Not for Me." Like the psalmist, feel free to ramble in the presence of God. The title sentence could take you in any number of directions.

Breakfast Muffins

I make these so often I don't have to refer to the original recipe,* which allows for even more play in the ingredients' list. (All white or wheat flour will work fine.) These muffins are not as sweet as some. You can always spread liberally with jam or butter.

1½ cups milk or fruit juice
1 or 2 eggs, slightly beaten
½ cup oil
¼ cup honey
1½ cups white flour
1½ cups whole wheat flour

1 tablespoon baking powder
½ cup uncooked oatmeal and/or
   wheat germ (I use ¼ cup of each)
¾ cup fresh or frozen (thawed) blue-
   berries or raisins or apples
¼ cup nutmeats (walnuts or pecans)

Preheat the oven to 350°F. With a fork mix the wet ingredients. Gradually add the dry and stir until mixed. Lumps are okay. Add the oatmeal, fruit, and nuts last. Put in greased muffin tins and bake 20–25 minutes. Makes 12 large or 18 small muffins. They freeze well. Serve warm or cold.

*Adapted from Mary Anna DuSablon's Cincinnati Recipe Treasury: The Queen City's Culinary Heritage (Athens: Ohio University Press, 1989), 161.

Who Ought to Be Coming?

Lord, what do You want me to do?
—ACTS 9:6, NKJV

ast weekend I started mentally gearing up to host a meal. What date? How many? Who? I've learned that a good dinner party includes people who share common interests but can also bring fresh ideas to enliven the table talk. I scribbled names of professional women with admirable faith, all lively conversationalists. The ideal grouping. I envisioned the perfect ladies' night.

Even the thought of entertaining can prompt me to tidy up. Skimming through and discarding old magazines, I stared at a bold-faced headline that made me think twice about the potential guest list: "Guess Who Ought to Be Coming to Dinner." I stopped and read the smaller print of the text by the Reverend Dr. Bonnie Thurston about Jesus and his "unacceptable dinner guests." She asked, "What if I invited folks to dinner and did not worry whether they belonged at the table?"[1]

The question reminded me of a Christmas party I organized years ago. I invited a number of social misfits. Most of them came. Some of them talked too much. Some hardly at all. They ate well and left full of cheer. Afterward I confided in a friend who knew all the others: "This gathering—I'm questioning my motives."

"What do you mean?"

"I invited them because I thought it might be their only holiday party."

Seeing kindness deeper than patronizing pity, he blessed the event. "That's not a bad reason," he assured.

I admit that I'm not quite ready to let go of my vision for the "ideal grouping." The invitation list is still in flux. But at least I'm thinking along different lines: Who ought to be coming to dinner? It's not a bad question to ask.

Lord, whether I'm planning a dinner or a day, help me to ask good questions, starting with "What do you want me to do?"

making it yours

1. If a schedule permits, give the guest list time to evolve. Write down names that come to mind, then gradually add and subtract as the Spirit gives you clarity.

2. Try to have a few backup names for a guest list, as some invitees may have schedule conflicts. Also, consider any guest's transportation issues as well as site accessibility. How can you as host, within reason, make the gathering doable?

3. Is "God, what do you want me to do?" the same as or different from the reflective question "What would Jesus do?" What, if any, distinctions do you see? How do those distinctions relate to your prayer conversation with God?

The Gift
Too Wonderful

. . . the surpassing grace God has given you.
Thanks be to God for his indescribable gift!
—2 CORINTHIANS 9:14-15, NIV

This story isn't mine. I heard it from my mother.

A woman with some stature and resources moved to a small town that had lost its luster. To get acquainted in the neighborhood, she hosted a women's gathering in her home—maybe a luncheon, maybe a tea. Wanting to honor her guests with her best, she brought out her valued china, linen napkins, and polished silver.

So far, so good. But the message intended was not the message received. Paul Tournier noted, "The gift which is too wonderful does not honour the one who receives; it humiliates."[2] The guests left the home tallying up the disparities between the contents of their cabinets—Melmac and stainless and Grandma's chipped luncheon plates—and the hostess's finery. They talked among themselves: *flaunting . . . putting on airs . . . not one of us.*

For all her efforts, through church and community activities, the hostess never broke through the barrier inadvertently raised that afternoon. No neighbor ever extended a return invitation to come for lunch or tea. This story saddened me when I heard it thirty years ago, yet I'm grateful for its memory: sometimes, depending on who's coming for dinner, it tempers my urge to set the table with too many silver spoons and forks.

And today it serves to remind me of the gracious wisdom of God, who chose to reveal Godself to us as an ordinary child—a crying baby, one of us. A gift indescribably wonderful, though presented in such a way that it would have been hard to recognize.

God, show me ways to honor, not humiliate, my guests.

making it yours

1. Reflect on your experiences as a guest. Can you identify times when you've felt "out of your league" or even humiliated? Have you possibly misread a hostess's intentions? How can these experiences help you become a more sensitive guest or hostess?

2. Similarly reflect on your experiences when hosting.

3. What does "thanks be to God for his indescribable gift" mean for you personally?

An Act of Hope

So now faith, hope, and love abide, these three.
—1 CORINTHIANS 13:13

O my God, relying on your almighty power, confiding in
your infinite goodness and mercy, and in your sacred promises,
I hope to receive pardon of all my sins, and grace to serve you faithfully
in this life, and life everlasting, through the merits of Jesus Christ,
my Lord and Savior. Amen.

—"ACT OF HOPE," TRADITIONAL PRAYER

Many Christians recite a three-part prayer that starts with an "act of faith," affirming, "Lord, I believe in you." It ends with an "act of love," avowing devotion for God and charity toward neighbors. As a hostess I've latched on to the descriptive phrase that's nestled in the middle of the prayer. It applies to every invitation I extend, but especially to one longtime friend.

Occasionally I invite her to come over for dinner—as part of a larger gathering that fills all the living room chairs and calls for extra leaves in the dining room table.

She always says, "Oh, you are such a good friend. Thank you for including me . . ." Then she pauses. I wait, hoping she'll say, "Yes, I'd be happy to come. I'd like to join the party." Instead, I often hear, "But no, I don't think so. Not this time." She's given me reasons for her reluctance: I have a small living room, in which she—a large woman—feels as if she's always "bumping into the furniture." I have small-framed dining room chairs, which she ever so kindly refers to as belonging in a dollhouse.

Because I have faith in my friend's goodwill toward me and faith in the integrity of our friendship, I don't take offense when she declines. I keep including her—as an expression of love. And here's where the title of the traditional prayer comes into play: for me, extending the invitation is an act of hope.

Like getting out of bed in the morning. Like opening a book or picking up the mail. Like praying to a God who welcomes my requests; unlike human friends, God doesn't seem to notice the imperfect furnishings.

God of hope, make me a person of hope. Today.

making it yours

1. At every turn—whether the task at hand is inviting, cooking, serving, or conversing—hosting relies on hope. What does this mean for you as you contemplate reaching out to others?

2. Consider the role of faith as it relates to your friendships, especially those that go "way back." In various relationships, are you mutually matched in your ability to know and experience faith in each other's goodwill and in the integrity of your friendship?

3. Compose your own prayer titled "An Act of Hope." It might well be startlingly different from the traditional prayer cited above, especially if it relates to welcoming others into your schedule and maybe into your home.

A Burden and a Pleasure

They've Grown Accustomed to My Ham

They went up to Jerusalem according to the custom of the feast.
—LUKE 2:42, NKJV

April was fast approaching. I was stressed with a looming work deadline. The house was neither clean nor tidy. My energy lagged. And yet . . . a set of friends had become accustomed to eating Easter dinner at my table. As much as I didn't want to lay out the spread, I didn't want to disappoint them. (In good faith I assumed they anticipated the event.)

Then again, my heart carried some accrued satisfaction from having established and hosted a holiday tradition: welcoming these particular guests, including Jane and Ken, who usually hosted me on New Year's evening; serving deviled eggs, pickled radishes, and my old-timey picnic ham that's increasingly hard to find in these parts.

Yes, I chose to make the phone calls: "I'd like to invite you here for Easter."

"Oh, thank you," Jane responded. "We'd love to come, though I must warn you. Ken hasn't been feeling well. He's lost his appetite. I don't know how much he'll eat or how long his stamina will last, but . . . if you can take us as we are . . ."

I visited or called five stores before finding one and only one smoked, uncooked pork shoulder, which I boiled for hours, then baked for more.

But on Easter Sunday, I set the full platter in front of seven guests, four "regulars" and three newcomers.

The gathering went particularly well. The church organist, coming off the most demanding week of his year, didn't nod off in the corner chair, as he sometimes has. Ken stayed long after the meal and engaged in the lively conversation. As they left, Jane whispered, "Ken hasn't eaten this well or been this animated in weeks. Thank you."

Within days scans showed how very sick Ken was. Hearing that news, I was especially gratified that I kept the festive tradition, searched for that ham. And sadly, Ken died the following October.

The time will come when I, like my mother before me, will say, "Enough. I don't have the energy to host a holiday." But not yet. God willing, I'm up for one more.

God, holiday feasts have always been important to your people. When I participate as a guest, give me a grateful heart. When it's my turn to host, please provide strength and a dash of joy as well.

making it yours

1. Think back over several years of major holidays. Are patterns evident—who hosts what seasonal gathering and where?

2. What aspects of your holiday hosting are burdensome? What aspects are pleasurable? If you're not satisfied with the expectations of others, brainstorm possible options—including shutting others out and eating alone. Do you think other options would reduce your burdensome stress? Your anticipated pleasure? What small changes could decrease your stress and increase your after-the-fact satisfaction?

3. Think of an upcoming holiday meal or gathering (or the preparations) as the subject of an artist's painting. Where is God in the picture? On the outside of the frame looking in? In the center of the scene? The cohost? The guest?

Picnic Ham, Boiled and Baked

A "picnic ham"—smoked pork shoulder—used to be a poor man's cut. In my region they're hard to find, apparently out of fashion, presumably because they're usually "ready to cook" rather than "fully cooked." But boiled and baked, a picnic ham is more colorful and flavorful than a precooked ham (rump). Some guests have asked if it was corned beef. The cut has a large bone and is fatty; figure buying one-half pound per person to be served.

Trim away the skin and most of its fat from a half picnic ham (about 5 pounds). Place it on a rack in a large stewpot. Cover the meat with cold water. Cover the pot and bring to a boil. Reduce heat and simmer, 15 minutes per pound. Remove from the heat and let steep in the hot water for 10 minutes. Carefully transfer the meat to a baking pan. Bake at 325°F at least an hour. Internal temperature should be 170°F, but I find that baking the ham longer, till it's quite crusty, just increases the flavor. Let sit before carving. Serve hot or at room temperature.

Refrigerate or freeze (or offer to your guests) the rich ham broth—for a lentil or bean soup base.

Adapted from Jean Anderson and Elaine Hanna, The Doubleday Cookbook: Complete Contemporary Cooking *(Garden City, NY: Doubleday, 1975), 385.*

A Step beyond Stone Soup

If all were a single member [a hand, a foot], where would the body be? As it is, there are many parts, yet one body.

—1 CORINTHIANS 12:19-20

'm not the only person in my church who walks into parish-hall pot-lucks eager to see and taste twenty dishes, each distinctly cooked and presented, even if they might all be variations on baked beans (as a friend claims to remember from childhood).

My church used to assign categories based on one's family name: A–H, main dish; I–P, salads; Q–Z, desserts. Where was the mystery? A committee hoped for more-specific clipboard commitments: "I will bring . . ." Where was the luck? I can still hear the guffaw when someone read my scrawled "God only knows." Now the parish table has loosened up, allowing for chance encounters. It's an anticipated event that gives chefs the chance to innovate, deli shoppers to repackage creatively.

As a child I was intrigued with the dynamics portrayed in the classic edition of *Stone Soup*.[3] How could the villagers not see that the stones at the bottom of the pot were a trick? How could they not know that the redcoats were teasing a town to be generous?

For years I connected the stone soup phenomenon with potluck dinners. In both situations everyone contributes something arbitrary to the mix of a meal. But the similarities are limited. Two servings drawn from a simmering soup might vary in their makeup—one containing more cabbage, carrots, or cauliflower bits than the other—but everyone's produce is similarly seasoned. The individual contribution, though vitally important, is not distinctly featured or enjoyed but incorporated.

Despite the perils of baked beans, the potluck spread has outlived the common-pot format. We humans like variety. When complaining of the monochromatic wilderness manna, the Israelites hankered for their Egyptian diet: "the cucumbers, the melons, the leeks, the onions, and the garlic" (Num. 11:5). We Americans value individuality. In its infancy the Jerusalem church held "all things in common" (Acts 2:44), but the model didn't prevail; we place more emphasis on Paul's picture of a variously membered community: a foot acting like a foot, a hand acting like a hand. To change metaphors: a mac and cheese tasting like a mac and cheese— laid on a table, nestled between a green bean casserole and a carrot salad.

Next Thursday when I step into my role as greeter-convener at a church potluck, I intend to add a new flavor to my prayer-grace: thanking God for the individual people who comprise our community, even as I thank the contributors for their discrete donations to our lunch.

Thank you for giving a scriptural reminder that you value individuality and the distinct contribution each of us "brings to the table."

making it yours

1. To organize a potluck gathering, what would be your venue? Time of day? A dessert course or an open array? Assigned categories or not?

2. Which mode of serving—and eating—do you prefer to plan? A one-pot meal or one with discrete taste opportunities? Give reasons that consider preparation and presentation.

3. Read Marcia Brown's classic (1947) edition of *Stone Soup*. Then have a conversation with God—and possibly friends—about its theme(s), including hospitality.

Take It Outside

[Adam and Eve] heard the sound of the LORD God walking
in the garden in the cool of the day.
—GENESIS 3:8

[Abraham] took curds and milk and the calf that he had prepared, and
set it before them. And he stood by them under the tree while they ate.
—GENESIS 18:8

Not so much these days—my friends complain of aching backs, weak knees, and insect aversions—but for years I enjoyed hosting picnics. Not the kind that required building a fire. Most often we didn't even locate a table but covered a patch of grass with a plastic liner topped with a cotton throw. Sometimes we set ourselves up within sight of an outdoor stage, anticipating a scheduled concert. Portable provisions. Sandwiches, salads, cold fried chicken, crudités, cookies. But it's not the fare that makes a picnic. It's the presence of food combined with the absence of walls. The sky is all yours. Nature's greenery isn't framed by small panes like an artist's landscape canvas.

In their retirement my parents visited me every spring. One sunny day I revived a pleasant childhood tradition by packing a basket and taking them on a lunchtime picnic. Ditto the next spring. Do something once, it's an adventure. Do it twice, it's a tradition. Before long they arrived with expectations. I felt a little pressure to perform, though maybe I was the one who upped the ante—boasting a new site each year: along a riverbank covered with daffodils, at an expansive pansy bed, in a sculpture garden, overlooking a high-flying fountain, on the Capitol lawn . . . I value a snapshot taken at our last expedition: my mom sitting in a wheelchair in the shadow of the Washington Cathedral. The bell towers looming over us were silent, but they might as well have been the belfries of all Christendom pealing loud and deep a song of peace on earth, goodwill.

When she was the kitchen boss, my mom thought we kids hyped the picnic experience; the fresh-air rewards weren't commensurate with the effort required by the inside-outside-inside haul. But she didn't realize that we'd remember the picnics best. Something out of the ordinary, though not as dramatic as Abraham hosting three unexpected guests whom he recognized and addressed as Lord. Something refreshingly godlike: breathing the garden breezes in the cool of the day.

Lord, whether it's picnic season or not, I choose today to delight in your created world and enjoy it in your presence and the company of others.

making it yours

1. Think of memorable picnics you've enjoyed. How old were you? Who were the hosts? What was the featured, favored food? Looking back on the day, do you appreciate their effort? Is a long-delayed thank-you note in order?

2. Though you can't replicate the old memory, consider planning an outdoor gathering. Picnics are especially appropriate when hosting children and strangers, people you may not feel comfortable inviting into your home. Consider your hassle quotient: The task of hauling might be an easier option than clearing the clutter from your dining room table.

3. Give some thought to one or more outdoor scenes in the Bible. (The Gospel of John features a number, including Jesus cooking a fish breakfast in chapter 21.) Allow the setting to draw you and your vision beyond the four walls of your home.

Dressing for Dinner

I will greatly rejoice in the Lord;
my soul shall exult in my God,
for he has clothed me with the garments of salvation;
he has covered me with the robe of righteousness.

—ISAIAH 61:10

Clothe yourselves with compassion, kindness, humility,
gentleness and patience.

—COLOSSIANS 3:12, NIV

Some people think that I overdress for Sunday worship. And, unless it's a spur-of-the-moment "come on by," when I'm hosting guests for dinner at my table, I gussy up a bit. A skirt. An accent of jewelry. Comfortable but well-chosen shoes. Maybe I picked this up from Margaret, the hostess of a New Year's weekend house party I attended throughout the nineties; long-established guests gave a quiet heads-up: "You'll want to 'dress for dinner.'" Or from my parents—who entertained frequently but usually on Sunday afternoons when we still sported our church clothes, including shoes freshly polished on Saturday night. Or maybe it's a throwback to "Let's play dress-up."

Over the years my guests have picked up on the signals. A few who used to arrive in T-shirts or summer shorts have bumped it up a notch. A breezy blouse. Simple capris.

I write this piece with a little ambivalence. Of course I want people to be comfortable in my home. And yet I mentally mark that there's something special about this meal laid out with guests in mind.

I look for scriptural parallels. In the Gospels Jesus speaks of God's heavenly banquet. "Blessed is the one who will eat at the feast in the kingdom of God" (Luke 14:15, NIV). In Matthew's account of a dinner parable, Jesus seems more concerned with what people wear to honor the occasion than with what they bring. And the Revelation 19 description of a "marriage supper of the Lamb" refers to the saints' righteous deeds being reflected in garments made of "fine linen" (v. 8). Isaiah says that God clothes us. Several epistles tell us to clothe ourselves. After dipping into a concordance, I get metaphorically confused, but nothing dissuades me from agreeing with Robert Farrar Capon, who proposes that "nowhere more than in good and formal company do we catch . . . the foretaste of what is in store for us" in the "celestial banquet."[4]

I'll continue to dress for church and dinner. Maybe not a flower in my hair but a tinge of blush on my cheeks and a bright scarf at my collar.

Lord, you serve as a model for any host: you accept us as we are,
even as you call us to be our best selves. As we serve others,
give us a vision for anticipating the banquet we will someday, in some way,
enjoy in your kingdom.

making it yours

1. What situation makes you more uncomfortable—being over-dressed or being underdressed compared to others in a group? How can this self-knowledge help you the next time you're staring at your closet, unsure of what to wear?

2. What category of dress do you envision wearing to the heavenly banquet (sweats, casual, business casual, formal, black tie)?

part 2

Stirring
the Pot

We often feel like we should be doing something else, something more important. I think it's a big problem with getting people to cook.
—MICHAEL POLLAN

Consider the Possibilities

Hear this, O Job; stop and consider the wondrous works of God.
—JOB 37:14

Thirty years ago at a company potluck, a coworker mused that there really were only ten or twelve basic recipes for cooks to tweak. It made a memorable conversation point. But if you spend any time reading recipes, you can see it's not that simple.

My favorite cookbooks are old—some older than I—and spattered and broken at the spine. They're rooted in the farmland of America, featuring ingredients available in a small-town, independent grocery. When contemplating a meal for guests, I'm often tempted to rely on old standbys. Beef braised in a soy marinade. Potato salad fortified by colorful chopped vegetables. Fruit pies. But in the early stage of meal planning, reading cookbooks can open a door to myriad possibilities—discovering a recipe to execute exactly or to modify loosey-goosey or maybe several to combine. Sweet potatoes whipped with orange juice and butter and a pinch of mace. An avocado condiment for hamburgers or slaw on hot dogs. Salmon loaf bulked with chickpeas. Before I close the book, I remind myself that having page after page of viable options and aisle after supermarket aisle of selections constitutes blessing upon blessing. Thank you, God.

There comes a time—standing in a grocery store, at a farm stand, or in front of my freezer—when I have to narrow the field. I make choices based on my budget, my guests' health concerns, my time constraints and mood. Beef or chicken? Buy lettuce or go with the cabbage tucked in the back of the refrigerator? Purchase dinner rolls and ice cream or make pumpkin bread and banana cream pie? But not yet. For a season my sometimes-narrow vision—stick to the tried and true—is as wide as the horizon on a flat prairie road.

Musing on the adage that variety is the spice of life, Methodist Bishop Edwin Holt Hughes proposes that "if we have not eyes to see the variety, we shall certainly not have palates to taste the spice."[1]

Open your eyes. Consider the possibilities for your menu. And for your creative talents, your ministry, your place among God's wondrous works.

God, increase my creative hunger, so that I may see the many possibilities
presented to me in the raw ingredients of your creation.

making it yours

1. When is the last time you tried a new recipe, new table or mantel decoration? Did the creative effort make you feel renewed or revitalized? If not, why not? Was the project too complicated? Is it time for something new and simple?

2. The quotation of Bishop Hughes is set in a Thanksgiving sermon. In that context, consider his reflection as it relates to your kitchen, your grocer, your garden or farmers' market.

served at my table

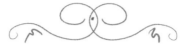

More Than Potato Salad

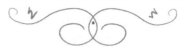

Gently stir together:

4 cups cubed, boiled potatoes (pref-
erably red, unpeeled)
½ cup chopped celery (1 rib)
¼ cup chopped green pepper
½ cup baby carrots, sliced like coins
¼ cup chopped onion
⅓ cup sweet pickle relish
2 tablespoons dry parsley

In a separate dish, stir or whisk:

6 tablespoons mayonnaise
1 tablespoon prepared (yellow)
mustard
1 tablespoon white vinegar
⅛ teaspoon black or white pepper
½ teaspoon salt (or to taste)

Gently stir the dressing into the potatoes and vegetables. Chill several hours
before serving. Serves 6.

Divulging Secrets?

The grace of the Lord Jesus Christ and the love of God and the fellowship of the Holy Spirit be with you all.

—2 CORINTHIANS 13:14

A few friends are coming for dinner tonight. While making coffee first thing this morning, I pulled out and flipped through several inches of splattered, disorganized cards and clippings jammed into an old three-by-five recipe box. I knew I would recognize the distinctive paper—the back of a bank deposit slip—before reading the heading: "Sardinian Thin Bread."

I'd copied the recipe thirty years ago while visiting a family friend on the West Coast. "This is very interesting. Could I have the recipe?" Louise said sure and handed me a page ripped out of a *Better Homes and Gardens* magazine. Later, I slipped the flatbread instructions into my recipe box, which itself has a story.

For my college graduation, my cousin Charlotte gave me a dime-store container with category dividers: casseroles, desserts, meats, vegetables . . . and about thirty of her workhorse recipes written in longhand: a starter kit that I've supplemented beyond the box's capacity. It now includes almost indecipherable lists scrawled by my mother, left behind in her estate.

Though I've never been denied, I hear of cooks who refuse to share recipes, usually claiming territorial rights, often loyalty to a family heritage: "I can't divulge the secret ingredient."

Do I have any recipes I'm reluctant to share? To be honest, I'm overly proud and protective of one (a Concord grape pie); just hinting at its required commitment—time and effort—discourages requesters. But mostly I'm honored to be asked. I'm happy to pass along my best.[2]

First Corinthians 11:23-26 puts the apostle Paul in this same category. "I received from the Lord what I also passed on to you," he notes, leading into a "recipe" for a spiritual meal. Giving thanks, Jesus took bread and broke it: "This is my body, which is for you; do this in remembrance of me." Jesus served wine: "This cup is the new covenant in my blood . . . drink it"; and in so doing, Paul says, we "proclaim the Lord's death" even to this day (NIV).

In the closing blessing of Second Corinthians, Paul reveals the not-so-secret ingredients that underlie our table fellowship with God and one another. On Sunday at an altar railing, my soul received its portion of grace and love. This morning when I opened my recipe box, my inner cook received hers.

Lord, my prayer today reflects Paul's handwritten blessing to one group of readers then passed along with kind intent: grace us, God, with your love, through Christ our Lord, in the fellowship of the Holy Spirit.

making it yours

1. If someone asks you for a recipe, how do you feel? How do you usually respond?

2. Name someone setting up housekeeping who might value receiving a collection of some of your time-tested recipes. In the gift package, include a newly written prayer or a copy of a classic prayer.

3. Reflect on Paul's Trinitarian benediction as a blessing you might extend to any guest you serve.

Through the Mail Slot

*Older women likewise are to be reverent in behavior,
not slanderers or slaves to much wine. They are to teach
what is good, and so train the young women.*
—TITUS 2:3-4

Amish and Mennonite cooks . . . their tutors have been
their own mothers and grandmothers.
—PHYLLIS GOOD AND RACHEL PELLMAN

Three years ago a young neighbor with special needs and disadvantages insinuated herself into my life. At my front door looking for daily attention, she would flip open the mail slot, align her eyes with the narrow slit, and scope out my living area. Harboring wild-eyed fear of my cat, she stayed outside, sometimes silent, sometimes stammering.

And there she was, Easter afternoon, a pair of brown eyes spying on my guests as they ate cheese and crackers. Half an hour later, craning her neck, she watched me, sitting at the end of the dining room table directing the flow of bowls and platters. Back in the living room eating pie, we all were aware of the metallic click as she'd run off, distracted, before returning to her eagle-eye perch.

I knew I was not powerless in the situation. I could have latched the screen door. Or asked her mother to call her home. But with a brief apology and explanation to my guests, I followed my heart: *Let her stay. She's unaccustomed to place settings and sitting in place. Let her see this ordered gathering. Let her observe how I host a meal.*

Three years older now, she walks around the cat in the living room. She grates cabbage for slaw and fills the pepper grinder in the kitchen. She sets the table when I'm expecting company. "Knife on the right." She looks puzzled. "You write with your right," I whisper.

Sometimes people ask where I learned to welcome guests. In a small-church parsonage I watched my mother prepare food and serve her large family and more—the parishioners and potentials my dad invited home. I watched my dad encourage conversations at multifamily picnics. As a young professional I watched colleague Marilyn orchestrate crowded-room buffets.

And now it's my turn to be shadowed. In the face of an opportunity I wasn't looking for—from the far side of the mail slot and now at my kitchen counter . . .

God, give me a vision for passing along to a younger generation what I've observed in and absorbed from older mentors.

making it yours

1. List names of women and men who taught you culinary or hosting skills. Identify the various kinds of expertise you have learned from these people.

2. No matter what your age, try to identify someone younger who can benefit from your growing body of knowledge/experience.

A Storied Recipe Compared to the Living Waters*

"Let anyone who is thirsty come to me, and let the one who believes in me drink . . . 'Out of the believer's heart shall flow rivers of living water.'"
—JOHN 7:37-39, NRSV

I walk into a church potluck carrying a hot dish that catches the attention of a puzzled diner. "What is it? Cheese?" Dan asks as he walks the buffet line. I take his question as an opportunity to tell him and anyone who will listen the story behind the recipe.

Ham and Mustard, as she called it, was my mother's only creative dish, baked slowly in a deep bowl. Not that it was original with her. She credited it to the husband of her rich, classy aunt, a school principal in faraway New York City. Uncle Henry was a househusband before the word had meaning. In my childhood the significant detail of his life was only whispered—ex-prisoner. Decades later we discovered his name in a 1920 *New York Times* local news feature: Henry, a professional "confectioner," convicted of burglary. My mother's aunt met him in the notorious Sing Sing prison, where she charitably volunteered. It seems he was paroled on the curious condition that the two get married. The *Times* implied that her job was in jeopardy, though she stayed on.

*See Gerard Manley Hopkins, "The Blessed Virgin Compared to the Air We Breathe," in *Poems and Prose,* ed. W. H. Gardner (New York: Penguin Classics, 1953), 54.

Mother's multiplied version of Henry's Ham and Mustard—more sauce than ham—tasted better than it looked; a thin and curdled gravy could easily smother enough mashed potatoes to satisfy our large family plus the parishioners Dad invited home for Sunday dinner.

The recipe Mom scrawled for me when I started housekeeping calls for a "handful" of brown sugar and includes the phrase "milk to cover"— the instructions as imprecise as the details of Uncle Henry's story.

Ham and Mustard is still famed countrywide by my siblings and cousins, even their children. A cousin serves it to senior citizens in Savannah. At Christmastime, it's the main attraction at my sister's table. I eagerly see, smell, taste from her deep casserole. "Hmm. Yum, but a little different, and lots of so-smooth gravy. What did you do?"

"Forget the slow oven." Microwave quickly. Whisk frequently. "And, oh, I doubled the sugar." How much does a recipe change from generation to generation? I asked more family cooks more questions. A sister-in-law adds butter and Worcestershire sauce and doubles the mustard but deletes the sugar. A cousin insists the ham be baked in a shallow pan, the ham slices snuggled side by side. My oldest sister prefers the sauce on bread, as a hot open-faced sandwich. Another sister? "I let the sauce cook down to flavor only the ham; I don't bother with a starch."

Maybe a storied family recipe is a little like the biblical "rivers of living water." British missionary Lilias Trotter, vacationing in the Alps, compared the movement of the Spirit to a picturesque glacial torrent: "obedient to its course in its narrow bed, yet just tossing with freedom and swing in every motion."[3]

Variations of the basic Ham and Mustard recipe are now serving fourth and fifth generations. Though it's been individualized by any number of cooks, the dish is recognizable and still attributable to its legendary source. Uncle Henry—not exactly the Holy Spirit, but comparisons do have their shortcomings.

Spirit of the living God, Source of our faith, thank you for this reminder that your outworking in each of us is personal and yet recognizably yours.

making it yours

1. Ask an older relative for any interesting stories behind family recipes. Write them down for the younger generation. It might be as simple as "served at Great-grandma's funeral."

2. Choose an old family recipe. Poll various relatives: How do they modify the original to suit their tastes and kitchen capabilities?

3. How have you experienced the Holy Spirit to be "obedient" to a narrow course and yet "tossing with freedom"?

---

served at my table

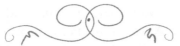

Uncle Henry's Ham and Mustard

Preheat the oven to 325°F. Cover the bottom of a greased 11 x 7 casserole or pan with:

1 fully cooked ham slice/steak (1 to 1¼ pounds) ½ inch thick, cut into 5 or 6 serving pieces

To make the mustard sauce: mix into a paste:
2 to 2½ tablespoons light brown sugar

2 tablespoons flour
1 tablespoon prepared (yellow) mustard
A few tablespoons milk

Add slowly and whisk:
1½ cups whole milk

Pour mustard sauce over the ham. If necessary, add a little milk to cover the ham. Bake uncovered 1 hour or until the sauce bubbles in the middle of the pan. Pour reduced pan juices over creamy mashed potatoes.

Let's Make a Contribution

I am going to Jerusalem bringing aid to the saints. For Macedonia and Achaia have been pleased to make some contribution for the poor among the saints at Jerusalem.
—ROMANS 15:25-26

My daughters don't *give*, they *provide*;
it's a different thing altogether, and, I would presume, not as satisfying.
—MOLLY O'NEILL, QUOTING "MRS. J."

Saturday mornings, whether I'm entertaining or not, a neighbor girl with special needs knocks on the door and makes a request (or is it a command?): "Let's make a recipe. Two recipes."

"Okay. Yes, come in," I reply. We've made pecan balls, meatballs, pumpkin cake, chicken soup, blueberry muffins, cranberry-orange relish in an antique food grinder, and more.

Last summer, while chicken á la king cooled in the skillet, we cut the crusts off bread slices (short strokes, so the bread won't tear) and layered on softened cream cheese and a cucumber "coin" to make tea sandwiches. "Chicken for the king. And party sandwiches for the queen," I joked.

"You can take some of these sandwiches home to your family, and I'll take some to my church for the after-service coffee hour," I said as we added the tip of a parsley leaf to the top of each cucumber slice. "That will be my contribution."

"What's that, Miss Evelyn? *Contribution?*"

Nothing like a child's question to focus one's reflections. "It's something you give—like a gift but not exactly. Something you give when you're working with other people on a project. I'll take cucumber sandwiches. Someone else will bring vegetables or cheese or brownies." I kept talking, maybe to myself. "When you're on a team, everyone contributes to the work. Like making the sandwiches. You peeled the cucumber. I cut it into coins that you placed on the cheese."

A year later the girl now accompanies me one Sunday afternoon a month to my church—an active member of the team that makes ham and cheese sandwiches. She counts and aligns bread slices for others to top with condiments. She and I pack the bags—a drink, a fruit, a sweet treat, two sandwiches—and send the meals off to be distributed in a downtown park. Driving home, I compliment her participation: "We make a good contribution to the team."

"Yes, we do," she says, knowing exactly what I mean.

Lord, scripture describes and shows your people as living in community, contributing to the common good. Show me what that means in my kitchen, in my ministry, in this season of my life.

making it yours

1. Identify ways in which your hospitality fits in to the work of a larger team or scheme.

2. If responding to number 1 was difficult for you, discuss church- or community-based options with a few other households. Brainstorm ideas and start small, with realistic goals (perhaps coffee hour once a month, a community dinner or senior citizens' lunch once a quarter).

Are You Protected?

She dresses herself [girds her loins] with strength. . . .
She looks well to the ways of her household
and does not eat the bread of idleness.
—PROVERBS 31:17, 27

I can still visualize my mom reaching her right hand around to the back of her waist to tug on a cotton apron string. As the half-apron started to fall, the same right hand rushed to the front center to grasp a fistful of percale. Finally she tossed the piece, like a rag though it wasn't, onto the back of a kitchen chair before walking into the dining room to host a meal. I can also remember laboriously ironing those aprons, some flowered, some calico, some with high bibs that covered her sagging bosom.

Then, for a generation, aprons went out of fashion. Clothing was cheap. Laundry was easy. Protective garments weren't chic. As Mary K. Mohler laments, some women "relegate [hospitality] to those who like to wear aprons and bake cookies."[4] Even so, I held on to a few and wore them until they were ragged. I've even made some as gifts—a full-front barbecue-type that a man might abide, not that I have any indication they're used.

But times are changing. Aprons are back. I've just unwrapped one—an early Christmas present—colorful paisleyed stripes at the bottom topped with French table linen. Almost too good to wear while cooking, though I will, as a portable towel, a defensive shield, a culinary statement: I'm on board, on site, and ready for work.

Proverbs 31 poetically details the activities and attitudes of an ancient female home manager. The Hebrew uses a strong phrase for her work-mode attire: "She gird[s] her loins with strength" (v. 17, KJV); she protectively hikes up her skirt so she won't trip. Centuries later the apostle Paul uses masculine warrior imagery to describe a spiritual preparedness: an armor that is largely defensive, including a "breastplate of righteousness" and a "shield of faith" (Eph. 6:14, 16).

What? Is this about heavy-grade, top-of-the-line aprons? Is this about making an intentional statement: I'm on board, on site, and ready to work?

Maybe so.

And if so, then count my mother and me in.

God, give me the desire and wherewithal to protect myself spiritually, especially as I work to feed those who await nourishment at my table.

making it yours

1. What is your work-mode attire? If not aprons, would wearing one feel like a step forward (with pride?) or backward to a bygone era you've left behind?

2. I've mentioned only two of the armor pieces cited in Ephesians. Others are a "belt of truth," shoes of the "gospel of peace," a "helmet of salvation," and "the sword of the Spirit, which is the word of God, praying at all times in the Spirit, with all prayer and supplication" (6:14-18). Reflect on this "whole armor" passage as it relates to the whole of your life and ministry.

   Which protective piece helps guard a particularly personal vulnerability?

3. Thinking of protection in broader terms, consider and reflect on this household metaphor: "A door has locks as well as hinges. Unless the door can be locked at certain times to nourish the family, the family will have little to offer one another or guests."[5]

The Prayer in My Work

*Aspire to live quietly, and to mind your own affairs,
and to work with your hands.*

—1 THESSALONIANS 4:11

My sister, hosting a holiday, puts me down to make the pies in her kitchen. "I've bought the crusts," she says. "You'll just need to fill them."

I pause before claiming my culinary territory: "Thanks, but I'll make my own dough," a special "never-fail" recipe, though on rare occasion it has.

Based on a few long-past mishaps, I don't deal with yeast. I don't have much patience for baking cookies. But I do enjoy making labor-intensive pies filled with fresh fruit thickened with sugar and flour from deep canisters. Rhubarb-strawberry. Blueberry. Apples peeled with a particular knife. I've been known to stop along a highway to pick unclaimed elderberries.

Last week a friend handed me three quarts of unshelled pecans. My young neighbor friend and I spent hours cracking the nuts and picking out the meats. I heard highlights of her school day. Sometimes we sang—"The Lord Is My Shepherd," "You Are My Sunshine," "Everything's All Right in My Father's House." We also worked in silence, peacefully anticipating the next c-r-aunch.

When I proposed that we make a pecan pie for her to take home, she parroted my noncommittal "I'll think about it."

When I said I'd found a recipe for a chocolate pecan pie, she exclaimed yes! And on Saturday we cut flour into shortening . . . rolled out a crust, crimped the edges. We melted chocolate, whipped eggs, added sugar . . . topped the pie with the biggest halves.

In the apocryphal wisdom book of Ecclesiasticus, Ben Sira describes the laborers—farmers, artists, ironsmiths, and potters; I'd like to add food pickers and parers, bakers and cooks—who ply nature's raw ingredients and "give solidity to the created world" (Eccl. 38:39a, JB). Their "prayer shall be in the work of their craft," an old translation says (DOUAY-RHEIMS, 38:39b).

Often enough when I am prepping for a meal, my thoughts are consciously focused on God. But even when they're not, I choose to think that I'm completing my culinary chores to God's honor, praising God with my resourceful efforts, saying thank you with my creative handiwork.

O Lord, may the work of my hands and the meditation of my heart be acceptable in your sight (see Ps. 19:14).

making it yours

1. Make something that requires raw ingredients and/or some hands-on assembling. As you complete the project, consciously turn your mind to reflection and prayer. Can you imagine that even your hands are praising or conversing with God?

2. Write a prayer in the voice of your hands, as if your hands were personified as "we."

Fruit Soup?

The fruit of the Spirit is love, joy, peace, patience, kindness, goodness, faithfulness, gentleness, self-control; against such things there is no law.
—GALATIANS 5:22-23

At that time in my spiritual life, I wasn't hearing the Lord's voice too much. But I imagined that if I could, he'd be telling me to just cook and not talk. I couldn't find any words that seemed right.
—VINITA HAMPTON WRIGHT

During Lent several local congregations join together for simple suppers—bread, salad, soup—followed by theological lectures. When our turn came around, our church set out a good spread. I made a potful of my old standby, vegetable beef.

At the end of the evening, diners inquired about recipes. At the end of the week, I received a formal e-mail from Coordinator Lisa. First the compliment: "The soups we offered this year were a big hit." Then the request: "Would you be willing to submit your soup recipes for publication in the church newsletter?" Lisa obviously wanted precise measurements and replicable results.

Oh dear, what should I say? I'd watched my mother make soup, and then I'd tried to improve the flavor. I sent a reply. First the appreciation: "Lisa, thank you for organizing the evening." Then the response: "NSR— No Such Recipe . . . it's a splash of this. A bunch of that . . ."

I could list ingredients that always land in the pot and contribute to the dish. But the amounts and even the proportions vary from batch to batch depending on how much supply I have on hand and how many people need nourishment. It often depends on how the Spirit moves as I assess and stir the pot.

When I consider the biblical list of the nine fruit of the Spirit, I sometimes wish scripture had given a specific, replicable formula: How much love? How much self-control? What's the proper proportion of peace to joy? But I'm learning that it's a case of NSR. How much of one or another depends on my spiritual readiness, the current need, and how the Spirit moves.

Holy Spirit, creatively work through me to produce a medley
of spiritual fruit.

making it yours

1. Make a pot of soup using nine ingredients from your current storehouse—pantry, refrigerator, freezer, garden. Without writing anything down, would you be able to replicate the recipe? Would you even want to?

2. Reread the biblical list of nine fruit of the Spirit. (Consider various translations; "goodness" is sometimes rendered as "generosity.") Looking back over the past year, what ingredient(s) has your life situation most required from God?

**Stirring
the Pot**

*Let us consider how to stir up one another to love and good works,
not neglecting to meet together, . . . but encouraging one another,
and all the more as you see the Day drawing near.*

—HEBREWS 10:24-25

Jesus, confirm my heart's desire
to work and speak and think for thee;
still let me guard the holy fire,
and still stir up thy gift in me.

—CHARLES WESLEY

A fter church this morning, I stopped by the home of my friend Sandra. She handed me a cookie, and we quickly caught up on personal news—some frustrations but mostly blessings commensurate with Thanksgiving week. Before I left we prayed for each other—for traveling mercies and hospitality's graces, for fulfilling days and restful nights.

Then this afternoon, as I pulled a cookbook off my shelf, I remembered what day it was. In recent decades the Book of Common Prayer has changed the set scriptures and prayers for today, the last Sunday before Advent. But traditionally in the Anglican Communion, the rector said a prescribed prayer (here slightly modernized): "Stir up, O Lord, the wills of your faithful people; that they, plenteously bringing forth the fruit of good works, may by you be plenteously rewarded. Through Jesus Christ our Lord."

And the Gospel reading? The feeding of the five thousand. The day came to be known as Stir-Up Sunday. And to dramatize the theme, cooks went home and started to whip up their favorite seasonal recipes—fruit-cakes, plum puddings, confections—preparing for Christmas.

Late afternoon I made pies—slipping one into the freezer for Christ-mastime. And I soon will head off to bed, mindful of my after-church conversation with Sandra, where we unwittingly commemorated Stir-Up Sunday by encouraging each other in our good and grateful works.

Holy Spirit, stir up your people—including me—to good and encouraging works of service.

making it yours

1. In the past six months, have you appreciated—or resented—the efforts of someone to "stir up" good works in you? Journal about or discuss your reactions.

2. The verses from Hebrews focus on a communal mutuality. In both a culinary and a spiritual context, consider ways to work to-gether with others to increase the scope or effectiveness of your hospitality outreach.

Salt to Taste

You are the salt of the earth.
—MATTHEW 5:13

Taste is a tool of faith—a sacrament, if you will. I think taste,
as well as the rest of the senses, fits the definition of a sacrament
as anything that serves as a visible means of divine grace.
—J. BRENT BILL

L ast evening a friend who's moving out of town emptied her freezer, handing me three roasted chicken carcasses. This morning I simmered and patiently deboned them, added onions, celery, corn, noodles, herbs. Promising nothing more than chicken soup, I impulsively invited a retired friend to join me in a few hours for lunch.

Anticipating her arrival, I stir and taste. Good but not great. More poultry seasoning and dill seed. Five minutes later, again. Still not right. I pick up my kitchen box of Diamond Crystal kosher salt and "add salt to taste," as the old cookbooks say. Not that I taste the salt itself but the heightened flavor of the other ingredients.

Setting the round box back in the cupboard, I read its promotional copy: "Why do renowned chefs swear that salt is the single most important ingredient in their kitchens?" I don't quite understand the answer, but if it's meant to startle, it succeeds: "Because salt is to taste what air is to breathing."

Salt has been valued since ancient times. Because they were "eat[ing] the salt of the palace"—on the royal payroll—Jerusalem's adversaries claimed they were obliged to bend the ear of the Persian king (Ezra 4:14). Roman soldiers received an allotment of salt, the origin of our word *salary*. In his May 1994 inaugural speech, Nelson Mandela envisioned a bright future for South Africa: "Let there be work, bread, water and salt for all."[6] In Central and Eastern Europe, salt and bread are goodwill gifts: may you eat and live well; may we commune as neighbors in peace. In the Middle East, salt's value as a preservative symbolizes covenantal bonds; we are brothers and sisters.

Colossians 4:6 exhorts Christians to "let your speech always be gracious, seasoned with salt, so that you may know how you ought to answer each person."

I don't quite understand the full effect of the apostle's metaphor, but if it's meant to challenge, it succeeds.

God, I see that I must let you season my life with salt,
which then becomes part of my being. Let there be "salt to taste,"
a well-proportioned amount that doesn't draw attention to itself
but draws out the fine flavors of my character.

making it yours

1. What is the single most important ingredient in your kitchen? in your spiritual life?

2. Consider times when you've cooked or eaten a dish that was so salty it was hardly edible. Or, conversely, times when you hankered for more salt in a tasteless dish. What insight do these experiences give you into Jesus' "You are the salt of the earth" or Paul's "Let your speech . . . be . . . seasoned with salt"?

The Root of It All

As you received Christ Jesus the Lord, so walk in him,
rooted and built up in him and established in the faith,
just as you were taught, abounding in thanksgiving.

—COLOSSIANS 2:6-7

My husband-and-wife guests tonight are friends who go "way back." Their respective dads were colleagues of my dad. They know the characters of my life. For a decade she invited me for dinner nearly once a week. We see each other less often now. But several times a year I invite them over, on short notice. In terms of food, I know what they like—and don't like. Tonight I'm serving meat loaf (a favorite of his) and homemade pickled beets (a favorite of hers).

Beets. Opening a sealed pint—the color reminiscent of Dad's roses past their prime—I remember my buying expedition last summer.

In the grocery express lane, a shopper broke the silence expected of strangers: "What are you going to do with all those beets?" Three big leafy bunches.

"Pickle them. Four pints. Every year I say I'm never going to do this again. It's such a hot, sticky mess. But here I am. My mother's recipe, mostly—pretty close."

I perceived that Mrs. Stranger wanted to hear more. "Mom wrote out precise amounts of sugar and vinegar and cooking time. But at the bottom she scrawled 'and spices.' What was *that* supposed to mean?"

"She's passed away?"

I winced. "Yes. My guests always raved about her pickled beets." Taste. Texture. A friend once ate a whole pint straight from the jar. Another turned down dessert, gingerly asking instead for more beets.

I restrained myself from telling more beet stories. Of the day Mother's pressure cooker exploded, shooting beet juice to the ceiling. Or of the neighbor girl who saw a small beet and asked, "What's inside it?"

Ahead of me in line, Mrs. Stranger pulled out her wallet—and a childhood memory: "One night my mom said she was *really hungry* for pickled beets. I didn't understand my dad's question: 'Are you trying to tell me something?' 'No!' When she'd been pregnant, she'd craved them. He was afraid . . ."

We chuckled. As Mrs. Stranger left the check-out lane, she turned around and waved. "This has been great fun—talking about turnips."

I smiled weakly. She didn't understand the look on my face—puzzlement that we hadn't been talking about beets, as I'd thought. The conversation had been all about roots.

Tonight at the table I will prime the table talk by telling this story. The conversation will take on a life of its own, jumping to supermarket strangers, the superior quality of farm-fresh vegetables, pregnancy cravings, Freudian slips . . . or maybe to our shared memory, shared roots.

Lord, you are the ground of love that nourishes our deepest roots.
Give us opportunity to appreciate the friendships, families, faith
communities, and even favorite foods that feed our growth.

making it yours

1. Consider a broad definition of *hospitality* that encompasses your shopping and an occasional grocery-store conversation with a stranger.

2. What does being rooted in Christ mean to you?

3. Whether hosting old or potential friends, how can you try to find common roots to help ground conversation?

part 3

Serving Up
Soup

*A meal is a feast not because any particular
amount of money has been spent or any
particular level of sumptuousness achieved, but
because time and care has been taken to make
this meal an event that all around the table can
celebrate together, taking pleasure in the food,
the company, the occasion—all of which, in their
own way, are foretastes of the kingdom of God.*
—MARGARET KIM PETERSON

Gracious Me? Gracious Me!

O LORD, be gracious to us; we wait for you.
Be our arm every morning,
our salvation in the time of trouble.
—ISAIAH 33:2

It isn't a woman's taste that makes a home peaceful and creative.
It is the woman herself.
—EUGENIA PRICE

For more than a decade, I annually planned and set out a buffet for a group larger than I could seat at my fully stretched table. One evening stands out in my mind: My friend John had come early to help me with last-minute kitchen details. Uncharacteristically, just minutes before others arrived, we both flashed, more angry with each other than we'd been in twenty years. In a silent fury I went upstairs, caught my breath, put on lipstick and heels . . . and came down to answer the door with a welcoming smile. The evening proceeded so well that John didn't understand my late-night "We've got to talk!"

"But you acted as if it had all blown over," he said. As if everything were copacetic.

"But I had guests at the door, a party to pull off." An event to make happen.

I remember other moments laden with stress. The rainy afternoon when I provided transportation to a guest who'd suffered a stroke: With me at his side, standing at his own front door, Richard tipsily leaned like the Pisa tower until we both tumbled, shaken but unhurt, onto the stoop. Was Richard up to this? Could he manage the steps to my place? Setting aside my liability worries, I asked if he wanted to proceed. Yes, he said. Let the outing begin.

And that same afternoon, when another older guest walking to the dining room inexplicably lost his grip on a half-full glass. "It's okay," I calmly assured while reaching for a leash to tether the cat away from the wet shards.

The evening the woman who'd agreed to bring appetizers arrived an hour late, empty-handed.

I like to think I value honesty, but sometimes practicing hospitality requires a different grace—tamping down one's stress for the comfort of the guest.

Proverbs 11:16 proposes that "a gracious woman gets honor." The biblical maxim can require a lifetime accrual. I trust I have years yet to bolster my account. For now it summarizes my prayer for you, for me, for one and all.

Lord, you have been gracious to us. Give us the patience and self-control to be gracious to others, whether in our homes, at work, or at play.

making it yours

1. Reflect on occasions when you've chosen graciousness over honesty for the sake of a guest at the door or table. Do you think you made a wise choice?

2. Think of the particularly gracious people you know. What characteristics can you identify? If appropriate, ask them for personal tips. Think of writing them an encouraging thank-you note.

3. Isaiah asks that God be gracious to Isaiah's people. List several occasions when God has been gracious to you and yours.

Try It? I Think You'll Like It

Oh, taste and see that the LORD is good!
—PSALM 34:8

Our lives are flavored by the renewed presence of God.
—MARGARET FEINBERG

When entertaining I tend to rely on a few favorite hors d'oeuvres recipes, chosen because they call for ingredients that I usually have on hand. One is a cheese ball bulked with saltine crumbs. Several are spreads for crackers or pita. A vegetarian pâté is especially tasty, though I admit that its brownish-green color may not look appetizing at first glance.

One evening I noticed that the meatless wonder wasn't receiving its due attention. *Hmm. This has happened before. They don't know what they're missing.* "Seeing is deceiving. It's eating that's believing."[1] I helped myself to a portion to confirm my recommendation. *Maybe I need to talk it up.* Hoping to break down my guests' resistance, I picked up the concoction and presented it to Jim, adding a little commentary: "This is a green bean and walnut pâté. Kind of unusual. Kind of nice. Want to try? See what you think."

Maybe just to be polite, he took a bit and then a bite. And then he smiled big. "Oh, yes . . ."

These days, while some people expend energy bad-mouthing God, a great many more just ignore God, not convinced that the Divine Being is worth their attention. After all, God's presentation isn't always flashy. God's hue is sometimes subdued.

My role as a hostess reminds me of my role as a faithful witness: by word and example to encourage others to taste and see—expect and experience—that the Lord is always and everywhere good.

> Say to every fallen brother,
> There's honey in the Rock for you.[2]

Lord, inspire and empower me to encourage others to discover your goodness.

making it yours

1. Do you, like me, have favorite recipes for dishes that taste better than they look? How can you heighten their appeal?

2. In what ways do you—or could you—present the goodness of the Lord to others who might not have noticed it among the world's many other offerings available to them?

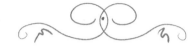

Walnut and Green Bean Pâté*

1¾ cups cooked green beans
¼ cup ground toasted walnuts (I use
a coffee grinder)
⅓ cup minced onion, sautéed in
1 tablespoon butter

2 tablespoons mayonnaise
½ teaspoon salt
¼ teaspoon black pepper
⅛ teaspoon nutmeg
2 hard-cooked eggs, chopped fine

In a blender whirl (not long, just until mixed) all the ingredients except the eggs. Stir in the eggs and refrigerate several hours. The consistency is more like a dip than a pâté. As noted, this tastes better than it looks. Serve with crackers or as a sandwich spread. Makes about 2 cups.

*Adapted from Mollie Katzen, The Moosewood Cookbook: Recipes from Moosewood Restaurant (Berkeley, CA: Ten Speed Press, 1977), 90.

All about Me?

"O LORD, please open his eyes that he may see."
So the LORD opened the eyes of the young man, and he saw.
—2 KINGS 6:17

A few years out of college, I boldly, hopefully, invited my boss and his wife, Linda, for dinner. I welcomed them into my two-room attic apartment, offered something to drink, and chatted amicably before retiring to the eat-in kitchen to put the food on the table.

Let's just say I hadn't yet learned the art of draining boiled potatoes. When Linda peeked around the corner—"Anything I can do to help?"—she caught me: thumb and forefinger picking hot potatoes out of the enamel sink. Envisioning myself in a comedy cast, I laughed. Linda didn't. Assessing the scene, she turned and quickly left the room.

Six months ago in an e-mail exchange with that former boss, I mentioned the memory: my embarrassment exacerbated by unshared laughter. Knowing his wife, he had a different take: "She's not judgmental that way, especially because she's dumped potatoes in the sink and the like many times." He reminded me of Linda's ancestry: "If she withdrew without saying anything, it was probably to help you (old Chinese response) save face." Oh? A kindness? The possibility hadn't crossed my mind.

More recently, clearing the table after serving guests, I noticed that a new, young friend, Allison, hadn't eaten much. To keep my energies focused on the dessert course and the after-dinner conversation, I chose to ignore an embarrassing thought: maybe the chicken was unaccept-ably dry, the salad excessively wet.

A few weeks later, I heard an Allison update: she was pregnant. Oh? Her appetite off-kilter? The possibility hadn't crossed my mind.

Lord, help me to see a world that is wider than my inadequacies.

making it yours

1. Think of a time when you might have (or know you did) misread an awkward situation, unnecessarily attributing an innocuous occurrence to your own inadequacies. What other factors might have contributed to the scene as it unfolded?

2. Have a conversation with God, asking for special grace to carry you through any upcoming hosting opportunities—grace to give all parties present, *including yourself*, the benefit of the doubt in any uncomfortable situations.

Color Counts

*Out of the ground the L*ORD *God made to spring up every tree*
that is pleasant to the sight and good for food.
—GENESIS 2:9

One March evening I invited Rhonda and Tim over for a dinner that promised to be tasty. Roast pork and honeyed potatoes. A pineapple and bread pudding/casserole. Cauliflower with white cheddar. Wilted cucumbers in sour cream. "It's ready. Come and eat," I beckoned. As I set the last serving dish on the table, I surveyed the culinary scene. *Ugh,* I groaned. "I'd get poor marks on this meal for 'presentation.'"

Tim was clueless. Rhonda caught my drift and filled him in: "A lesson in junior-high home economics: a featured menu should be multicolored."

"Right!" In jest I tried to justify the monochromatic theme. "It's Lent, you know. At church that means no flowers at the altar. Just green leaves." But as a hostess I wasn't in a Lenten frame of mind. From the ledge of the refrigerator door, I quickly retrieved a pint of pickled beets. "Let's add this," I suggested, setting the "side" in the middle of the table. "And wait till you see the dessert," I said as I pulled out my chair.

"Color is . . . in brief terms, the type of love," wrote John Ruskin.[3] His context was the birth-and-death tones of nature: dawn and dusk, springtime and harvest, blossom and fruit, the beginnings and endings and beginnings that cycle round, year upon year.

I won't go so far as to claim that a colorless meal is a loveless service, but I've never again laid out before guests such a pathetically pale dinner. One preventable "oh dear" was enough. It's about more than nutrition.

"What brightens the eye gladdens the heart" (Prov. 15:30).[4] And my heart says that color counts.

God, thank you for the wide, wild array of nourishing and beautiful foods you've created and for the bounty that is ours to serve and enjoy.

making it yours

1. If you note a dearth of color in a meal, what pantry items could you quickly pull out to fill the gap?

2. If "what brightens the eye gladdens the heart" rings true for you, dwell on and thank God for one such good memory.

3. Get outside and enjoy the seasonal colors—the creation that is "pleasant to the sight."

Bread, Baked and Broken

Taking the five loaves and the two fish, [Jesus] looked up to heaven and said a blessing over them. Then he broke the loaves and gave them to the disciples to set before the crowd. And they all ate and were satisfied.
—LUKE 9:16-17

Their eyes were opened . . . in the breaking of the bread.
—LUKE 24:31, 35

don't make yeast bread, nor did my mother. But it was my paternal grandmother's specialty. When I think of our summer visits, I don't remember loaves for slicing. We all anticipated her smooth-topped, tennis ball–sized rolls, all abutted in a low, round pan. Her recipe was imprecise (lard the size of an egg). And her bun-forming method was impossible to replicate. In a bygone kitchen accident she'd cut off the top knuckle of her left index finger. And that stubby digit played a critical last-minute role, tucking in the underside dough as if it were a dumpling encasing a small golden apple. As a toddler I thought the mangled finger affected or effected the unique product—and maybe it did. Though she tutored her daughters, their offerings never tasted like Grandma's Buns, which we tactilely split open with opposing thumbs and slathered with homemade jam. Mum, as my grandmother was called, died when I was a teen. Her physical presence is a distant memory. I was the guest. I recognized her as the hostess with wounded hands and salubrious gifts.

We know Him in the breaking of bread, and we know each other in the breaking of bread, and we are not alone any more.[5]

All five synoptic Gospel accounts of Jesus miraculously feeding crowds describe him as taking bread in hand and breaking it. It's a physical action that seems foreign to our modern prepackaged "sliced, please." The phrase "breaking bread" has morphed into a metaphor for sharing a physical or spiritual meal.

My dad's favorite Gospel story—the text of his last sermon—shows Jesus again breaking bread, this time at a friend's dinner table. That afternoon on the road to Emmaus he and said friend Cleopas have seemingly happened upon each other, though Cleopas thinks he is walking with a stranger who hasn't heard the week's news: about the crucified prophet and now his missing corpse. Even hearing Jesus' scriptural interpretations, Cleopas remains clueless until the man he invites to stay for supper takes a lead role—picking up, blessing, and breaking the day's loaf. As recorded, it isn't Jesus' profile, gait, cadence, or teaching that prompts recognition. Cleopas notes something unique and sacred in Jesus' hands. Does he see nail prints? Or something more familiar from earlier days— the way he handles bread? I propose that as Jesus broke bread, host Cleopas recognized the wounds and the gifts of a guest.

God, whether I'm a hostess or a guest, I'm breaking bread with wounded but wonder-working companions. Open my eyes to see the message revealed in their broken or breaking hands.

making it yours

1. Identify various aspects of a host's or guest's life story that might be evident in his or her hands (for instance, crippling arthritis, gnawed nails, oven burns, farmwork scars). Consider how these hands can help you see the wounded Christ in others.

2. In the story of Cleopas, the guest momentarily became the host. If Christ is a guest at your table, how might he also be serving as host?

"Martha, Martha"

Martha was distracted [KJV: cumbered] with much serving.
And she . . . said, "Lord, do you not care that my sister [Mary] has left
me to serve alone? Tell her then to help me." But the Lord answered
her, "Martha, Martha, you are anxious and troubled about many things,
but one thing is necessary. Mary has chosen the good portion,
which will not be taken away from her."
—LUKE 10:40-42

Long story, but I offered to organize an outdoor party, celebrating a friend's accomplishments. About fifty people were expected. My role included shopping for table supplies, cooking and transporting salads, staging the event in a public park. The day before the picnic I talked to a guest who was buying the sliced beef. Apparently hearing stress in my voice, he said, "Evelyn, it's all going to come together just fine. Don't worry."

What? I was speechless. It would—and did—"come together" because I made it happen. Stayed on point. Worked my tail off. Went home exhausted.

I naturally resist facile applications of Jesus' mild rebuke, "Martha, Martha . . ." as if her "much serving"—much work—was itself a problem. I remember my dad's great perplexity—"What's the big deal?"— over my aged mother's increasingly intense refusal to host a full meal for anyone except family. "I just can't do it anymore." Those gender-role dynamics make me wonder if Martha was tempted to tell Jesus that he could go make his own dinner, maybe multiply his own fishes.

I spend more time with this scripture story and note that Jesus doesn't reproach Martha for her efforts but for her mind-set; he doesn't "Martha, Martha" the work of her hands but the tenor of her heart. The exchange might have happened in any context—not related to a hostess's table.

This morning in the fog between sleep and wakefulness I imagined Jesus speaking to me grievedly, as he did to Martha: "Evelyn, Evelyn, you are . . ." I allowed the Spirit to remind me of my besetting distractions, anxieties, fears.

My response is to repeat a centuries-old prayer for purity (Book of Common Prayer) that I hear every Sunday before my congregation gathers at the Lord's well-laden table:

Almighty God, to you all hearts are open, all desires known, and from you no secrets are hid: Cleanse the thoughts of our hearts by the inspiration of your Holy Spirit, that we may perfectly love you . . . through Christ our Lord.

making it yours

1. When you are "cumbered with much serving," what emotional or spiritual "checks" can you have at hand to help you stay centered and poised, your heart in a Christ-centered mode?

2. If the Spirit were to "Martha, Martha" you, what might the mild rebuke be about? How would you respond?

My Dad Never Taught Me . . .

[God] has caused us to be born again to a living hope through the resurrection of Jesus Christ from the dead, to an inheritance that is imperishable, undefiled, and unfading, kept in heaven for you.

—1 PETER 1:3-4

E very summer my parents hosted multifamily picnics, organized on short notice and by phone: "Bring meat to grill and a dish to pass." My mother made one or more salads to prepare for these backyard events. My dad took charge of the outdoor cooking. From the garage he pulled his grill and a gallon-sized tin can jerry-rigged like a chimney. He crumpled newspapers in the bottom of the contraption, mounded charcoal (he disapproved of briquettes) on top, and set it ablaze. Twenty minutes later, sweat dripping down his jowls, he flipped burnt burgers and turned blistered hot dogs. Women cooking in the kitchen, men grilling outdoors. This was the way God or maybe the Pilgrims or Betty Crocker meant the world to be.

On my own years later, I hosted a picnic without the benefit of a spouse or a yard. Suggesting we meet at a county park, I invited two couples. "Be my guests," I said, which meant I'd provide the accoutrements and food, including meat to grill on the small hibachi I stored on my stoop.

I had no intention of grilling. I knew the two men would step forward to light the briquettes and wield the spatula. But I was wrong. "You guys must be better at this than I." Didn't work. "My dad never taught me his secrets." No dice. I remember my confused disappointment at the end of the evening as I doused the coals with water I'd drawn from a fountain, and later as I gingerly maneuvered the hot hibachi into my car trunk. I've since hosted more picnics but none that involved raw meat or fire.

It took several more missteps before I learned to rein in my expectations of hands-on help from guests. ("How about moving conversation to the front steps—and husking this corn?" Stares and silence. Are you kidding?) But at that park-picnic venue a reality registered: my familial gender-based patterns are not universal laws of nature.

The heritage I received from my parents includes so much that I value: their ministry concerns, their integrity, their frugality. The closing paragraphs of their last will and testament quoted the apostle Peter's description of a spiritual, imperishable inheritance that would outlive, outshine anything else they could offer us. That's the legacy I most dearly claim.

God, even decades after I've left my parents' home, their household patterns influence mine. Show me which ones deserve to be valued and which ones need to be set aside—for the comfort of my guests and the alleviation of my stress.

making it yours

1. Especially in terms of the domestic arts, what familial patterns do you value? What patterns have you tried to overcome or get past?

2. Consider writing a few paragraphs concerning your legacy for the next generation. What spiritual and household "inheritance" do you hope to leave to your family members?

Last Comforts

As a mother comforts her child,
so will I comfort you.
—ISAIAH 66:13, NIV

Then Jesus told [the girl's parents] to give her something to eat.
—LUKE 8:55, NIV

It was the second distress call in a week from Anne, an elderly neighbor whose mind was shutting down, her life closing in. Fear and frailty had forced her to sign papers that opened doors to a nursing home placement, not that her heart was ready to leave her trim and tidy apartment. "Please come up here," she said tearily on Monday afternoon. "They say I have to go tomorrow." For an hour, until an aide arrived and assured me that the move was soon but not imminent, I brought mementos and snapshots to her side. I let her reminisce. I combined two photo albums into one. On a bureau we set out keepsakes for her to take.

The same call came two days later, midafternoon. "It's tomorrow morning," she reported, panicked. This time I had outside confirmation. Yes, this would be Anne's last night in her home. As I hiked up the hill, I asked God for direction: "Show me what to do and say" in this vacuous hour until the evening aide arrived.

Anne wouldn't let me pack clothing into a suitcase. She didn't want to talk about the past, and the future churned up double, double boiling trouble. All I could think to do was to address the physical need of this present moment. Knowing she'd been disparaging her aides' culinary offerings, I assessed the contents of her refrigerator and cupboards and posed a question my mother had occasionally asked me: "What would taste good for dinner?" I'd found a russet. "A baked potato?"

When I left that evening, Anne's spirit was tempered. With her aide's help she was eating a flaky potato topped with butter and sliced black olives. "A little more pepper?" Yes. A few spoonfuls of broccoli. Diced chicken sprinkled with poultry seasoning. She seemed to be enjoying the taste if not the reality of the last dinner of her independent life. Not that she remembered my effort even for a day. The next morning Anne called to tell me she was moving away—as if this would be news.

But I won't soon forget the experience. My memory of the question I thought to ask—what would taste good?—continues to increase my confidence in the Spirit's ability to whisper a timely, present-tense word.

God, today, any day, bring to my mind phrases that when verbalized and acted on bring comfort to your children, whether that means my neighbor, a stranger, or even me.

making it yours

1. Think of your own comfort foods and treat yourself—in moderation of course.

2. In what way can you show hospitality to someone who is housebound or limited in the ability to care for himself or herself? Make a plan to reach out and serve this person sometime in the next month.

3. Mentally review times when you've felt that the Spirit gave you the right words to say at the right time. Say or write a prayer, thanking God for that special grace.

Serving Strangers

I was hungry and you gave me food, I was thirsty and you gave me drink, I was a stranger and you welcomed me.
—MATTHEW 25:35

Do not neglect to show hospitality to strangers, for thereby some have entertained angels unawares.
—HEBREWS 13:2

I was young and single. My siblings were married with families. I was traveling to my parents' for Christmas, just the three of us for the twenty-fifth, though more would gather in for turkey with trimmings later in the week.

Early in December my dad phoned: "If I could arrange it, how would you feel about our eating Christmas dinner at the county jail?"

Are you serious? I knew what he was thinking. Charles Colson, founder of Prison Fellowship Ministries, had recently quoted an inmate who'd claimed that volunteers eating lunch with him had been the most significant part of an in-prison seminar. My dad wanted to redeem our low-key holiday with dramatic service.

Then and there my best offer was "I'll think about it."

A week later I counterproposed. I couldn't handle Christmas in a jailhouse, but if he wanted to reach out to strangers, I'd be willing to eat at a nursing home.

Not enough drama? Too threatening at his age? The subject was dropped. On Christmas Day I gathered vegetables from their cold cellar and simmered a hearty venison stew, served up to us three.

The Greek word (*philoxenia*) translated "hospitality" in the New Testament refers to our showing goodwill to strangers. Yikes. I'm more comfortable with friends, fellow worshipers, and maybe acquaintances, friends of friends. The first century was a less dangerous time and place, or so we're told. Here and now, we might serve strangers in our church basements or at barbecue fund-raisers. We might hand out canned goods at a food pantry, deliver meals-on-wheels, or pay for someone's diner breakfast. We might invite international university students for Thanksgiving dinner (and hope that it's a onetime commitment). We're a risk-averse and self-protective culture, with good reason. Welcoming strangers, *especially* those who don't come with firsthand character references—again, I say yikes.

I serve cautiously, with others. At my church I help make and pack sandwiches for a street ministry. Just last week I walked through the delivery process in two city parks. Asking no questions—any comers welcome—I handed out white paper bags, each holding two sandwiches, a fruit, a cookie, a water. Another volunteer, John—whose regular partner just happened to be home ill—followed with homemade soup. Slightly self-conscious, I'm not sure why, I looked into scores of weathered or wakeful faces and too quietly said, "Bless you."

"Thank you." "Thank you very much." Considering Matthew 25 and Hebrews 13, I can't venture who opened any of the ham sandwiches I distributed. Jesus? An angel? Men and women walked away, toward picnic tables or parking curbs, some eating in groups, others alone. I noted a community spirit: a weathered man guiding a younger brother, visually impaired, through the distribution and to a table. Though we didn't seek evaluations, the soup received thumbs-up approval.

"It was a good night," John said, driving back to my car, "everyone under control," meaning sometimes some aren't.

There was nothing dramatic about the hour. The next night and the next, many of the same characters gathered to wait for another bagged meal. And winter's closing in.

I don't know. I may never run the route again, or maybe yes because of John's positive assessment of his volunteer role: "It's like serving at a banquet that I don't have to cook."

God, show me—introduce me to—ways by which I can serve strangers, especially those who are living precariously on the edge of the community.

making it yours

1. Describe your comfort level when considering opportunities for eating with and/or serving food to strangers.

2. With whom might you join forces to serve people living on the edge in your community?

Reclamation Declaration

[Jesus] told his disciples, "Gather up the leftover fragments, that nothing may be lost."

—JOHN 6:12

A s one of many houseguests who had enjoyed a capon dinner the previous evening, over breakfast I made an offer I was sure the host would not refuse. I spoke hopefully: "May I tear down the carcass and make soup?"

He seemed surprised at and unimpressed with my suggestion. "What? No thanks. It's already in the trash."

Now I was the one to exclaim, "What?" *Doesn't everybody . . .* In my parents' home, and mine, any fowl's roasting called for a reprise, an aromatic simmer followed by a delightfully tactile deboning that resulted in a savory dish. I gulped a mouthful of coffee. *What a missed opportunity—in my estimation worth every bit of the kitchen mess.* (Was I being judgmental? At the time I couldn't see it.) Jesus himself, after feeding a crowd, asked his disciples to gather up the leftovers, not just to clean up the littered hillside.

That conversation years ago heightened my resolve on a recent Thanksgiving as I set out a golden twelve-pound turkey and two fruit pies, to say nothing of mashed potatoes and stuffing and vegetable sides. All this to serve four diners. After dessert we filled plastic containers with leftovers for my friends to take home, with ample for me too. That evening I closed the refrigerator door on plenty of potential. There it chilled until Friday afternoon, when I pulled out the carcass, boiled and stripped the bones, added onions and celery . . .

Anticipating the occasion, I'd put my name on the church's roster to deliver dinner Friday to a housebound couple. I stayed to eat with them, serving up my turkey-corn soup, not quite as hot as it should have been and in need of a pinch of salt, but fine enough fare—an amateur attempt to, like Christ, reclaim what might have been lost.

God, I don't want to be wasteful. In my shopping, cooking, serving, storing—help me see ways to rightly use the resources you've so graciously provided me.

making it yours

1. Imagine what the disciples did with the "leftover fragments" from the miraculous feeding. How can this detail of the Gospel story inform or direct the way you serve neighbors, strangers, guests?

2. Say you've prepared too much food for any occasion. List various viable options for serving it up.

Chicken- or Turkey-Corn Soup

See the earlier "Fruit Soup?" meditation about imprecise soup recipes. Proportions here can be significantly modified, depending on ingredients at hand. If you're starting with a roasted carcass, break it into manageable sections and boil/steam it, covered, in 6 cups of water, for 20 minutes. With tongs remove the bones from the broth. When you can touch them without burning yourself, debone the meat. Place meat scraps back in the 6 cups hot broth and proceed.

1 cup chopped onion, sautéed
1 cup chopped celery, sautéed
6 cups chicken or turkey broth (see note above)
2 cups cooked chicken or turkey chunks/scraps
1 chicken bouillon cube (optional)
1½ cups canned or frozen corn
1 bay leaf

1 teaspoon poultry seasoning
¾ teaspoon dill seed
1 teaspoon salt
½ teaspoon black pepper

Mix together and simmer for 20 minutes. Then add:
1½ cups wide egg noodles
3 tablespoons dried parsley

Simmer 10 more minutes, or until noodles are cooked. The soup will be thick. Add hot water if needed. Adjust seasonings to taste. Serves 6.

part 4

Sitting
at Table

*When we break bread together we leave our
arms [weapons]—whether they are physical or
mental—at the door and enter into a place of
mutual vulnerability and trust.*
—HENRI J. M. NOUWEN

The Candle in the Corner

In your light do we see light.
—PSALM 36:9

A brass candleholder sits on a ledge in my living room—within sight of my dining room—where it unobtrusively supports a short white candle. I strike a match and light the wick only on special occasions: just as company arrives for dinner. No one ever seems to notice the solitary flame, protected from drafts by a glass chimney. I see it differently.

The light's container connects me to my natal family; it was one of my parents' seven distinct brass candlesticks, each a different height and form, each representing one of their children. In the estate, the tallest went to the oldest; mine is one of the smaller—not that I feel shortchanged.

The burning wax ties me to my faith community. I don't buy new candles but pick up giveaway stubs that have blazed out their first half-life at the church, at the altar.

Then there's the fire itself. Last night it caught my eye soon after seven girlfriends settled around a tray of hors d'oeuvres set on the coffee table. When Friend A noticed the stress of Friend B over hospitalized Friend C, she offered a suggestion: "Could we just stop and pray, right now?"

All agreed, and I took the lead.

Before I closed my eyes, the sight of the flame drew my spirit toward God's gracious light shining in our midst. After the "amen," it seemed the reflection of the candle in a mirror against the far wall confirmed my guests' place in the good company of God's large family—and consequently mine.

Lord, may my family and home, like a brass candlestick, hold your gracious light as it shines on, in, and among my guests.

making it yours

1. Consider lighting a specially placed candle when guests arrive, reminding yourself of God's presence in your midst.

2. If conversation reveals a guest's personal distress, what might you do to alleviate the stress among the other guests?

To Pray or Not to Pray?

*Every good gift and every perfect gift is from above,
coming down from the Father of lights.*
—JAMES 1:17

Give thanks to him; bless his name!
—PSALM 100:4

My guests one night weren't believers. Before they arrived, I puzzled over the question: to pray or not to pray before the meal? I admit, I don't always stop to thank God for food that I eat alone, so why should I, would I want to, need to, say grace when others gather at my table?

The Gospels show Jesus himself blessing the food he was serving to others. Christians picked up the Jewish pattern, praying extempore or repeating memorized lines. Though unsubstantiated, a story prevails that Josiah Wedgwood gave John Wesley a large teapot imprinted with a poetic table grace composed by John Cennick, a fellow evangelist:

Be present at our table, Lord;
    be here and everywhere adored;
thy creatures bless; and grant that we
    may feast in paradise with thee.[1]

Spoken or sung, the prayer remains popular today.

As a five-year-old, my niece Elizabeth explained the reason for her family's mealtime custom: "We hold hands so we don't eat while we pray." Her analysis—*she needs a hands-on reminder to give God full respect*—influenced my decision: at my table I would remind myself as well as my guests of what is important to me.

When everyone was seated at the table, looking to me for a go-ahead, I said I would like to pause for prayer. I didn't suggest any hand-holding regimen. I just articulated a simple thank-you "for these friends and this food, for this fine day. And be with us now, through the evening. Be present at this table, Lord. Amen."

As I raised my head, I heard the slightest grunt of approval.

With a smile I passed the potatoes—to the right is right. "Help yourselves." Let the meal begin.

Lord, thank you for small opportunities to show my respect for you among my friends.

making it yours

1. In what, if any, situations do you think grace before (or after) a meal would not be appropriate. Why?

2. As a child or adult—at home, at church, at Scouts—have you memorized any table graces? Consider their appropriateness for nonfamily guests or group functions.

3. Would some tangible reminder of the importance of "grace" help you remember to pray and to pray with due respect?

Turning the Table

Behold, I am doing a new thing;
now it springs forth, do you not perceive it?
—ISAIAH 43:19

W hat's this about?" Skimming through the dining section of etiquette books I discover an old phrase. It's apparently a traditional hosting responsibility that isn't necessary in informal family-style dining, where everyone at the table is actively or passively attuned to a single conversation.

But consider other scenarios. My friend Shay grew up in the 1930s in an English manor house, which suggests wide tables with formal settings: candlesticks and tureens that obstructed one's view. Or think of those banquet-sized wedding-reception tables where strangers on the far side might as well be seated across a street.

Sometimes whole-table conversations are impractical or undesirable; the etiquette books give a name to the art of a hostess talking for half the meal with the diner to her right and then consciously disengaging, to then focus her attention on the person to her left. If things go according to the book, the conversational groupings of the entire gathering shift, thus "turning the table." Gregarious guests have occasion to regale a new set; tongue-tied introverts, to prove their mettle. It's a twist on the familiar reversal-of-fortune idiom, turning the table midgame when playing backgammon or chess: a near-winner gets a new challenge; an almost-loser, a second chance.

In Isaiah, God, maybe like an old-school hostess, says, "I am doing a new thing." The statement is followed by a question: "Do you not perceive it?" *Do you get it? Good can come of this.* Today, mulling over a new context of an old phrase, I see that it takes an *optimistic* mind-set to accept change as an opportunity, not a threat. Over the years, with the help of friends and nudged by the Holy Spirit, I've learned to name and claim some positive personal qualities: creativity, punctuality, responsibility, thoughtfulness. I can't say that the *O* word has ever made the list. Maybe it's time to turn . . .

God, your Word says that you set change in motion even as you ask us to amend our mode of response. Help me, help us, to be open to the challenge of change.

making it yours

1. How can the obscure etiquette phrase "turning the table" guide you in facilitating conversation at your table or in more informal contexts?

2. How can the phrase help you accept positive change in your life—even with an optimistic mind-set?

Table Talk

Listen, children, to a father's instruction, and be attentive,
that you may gain insight; for I give you good precepts.
—PROVERBS 4:1-2, NRSV

Dear Miss Manners:

My parsonage parents frequently entertained. After dessert
my father gestured toward the living room and predictably
said, "Let's find more comfortable chairs." I've recently
attended dinner parties where we sit at the table for three
hours or more, until a guest intimates fare-thee-wells. It just
feels wrong on two counts: for the guest to suggest the move
away from the table and for the party to progress from the
dining room straight to the foyer.

Though Miss Manners kindly, generically acknowledged receipt of
my e-mail, she didn't address my concern, which means I've looked
elsewhere for opinions if not expert clarity. I admit my ulterior motives:
trying to prove myself right and others wrong.

My friend Jane quotes her mother's standard line: "Let's go into the
living room." Camilla suggests a situational approach: it depends on
how many bodies and how many living room chairs. My sister appreci-
ates Dad's tack but suggests it harks back to his childhood, when the

men retired to the "front room," while the women lagged behind. A brother mentions a contrary precedent, Martin Luther's long-winded "table talks." With a laugh, Mary suggests keeping guests at the table after dessert. Away from the table, God only knows what would happen, their being so addicted to connectivity—texting their messages, confirming their statuses, checking their feeds—"Back to my phone: The market's down. The meal was great. Got to go."

Online I did find an authoritative voice who pronounced that "the hostess . . . suggests that everyone go into another room for coffee and after-dinner drinks."[2] Ah, vindicated; thank you.

I've spent entirely too much effort trying to justify my family's tradition. And yet I've made good use of the temporary obsession. My father's practice—right or wrong? archaic or timeless?—has provided several rounds of dinner conversation that ran their natural course, no one feeling compelled to shut down the room with a line I've come to dread: Let's google it.[3]

"Blessed is the one who . . . gets understanding" (Prov. 3:13)—in face-to-face fellowship, whether at the table or in more comfortable chairs.

God, show me ways to weave the threads of my life into the conversations in my home.

making it yours

1. Mentally have at hand a few family stories—maybe quirky traditions or memorable phrases—that can help you as a host or hostess to facilitate conversation, especially with people you don't know well. Don't set yourself up as an authority; just encourage participation.

2. Consider Proverbs 3:13. Write a prayer asking God's help in gaining understanding of yourself, your family heritage, God's world, and these times. Ask God to work through lively table conversation.

On My Mind: Augustine's Rhyme

With [the tongue] we bless our Lord and Father, and with it we curse those who are made in the likeness of God. From the same mouth come blessing and cursing. My brothers [and sisters], these things ought not to be so.

—JAMES 3:9-10

It seems some social hazards of gathering people together never change. A Latin inscription attributed to Saint Augustine has been found in the ruins of a twelfth-century monastery, presumably in a dining room. Translated it reads: "Who injures the name of an absent friend, may not at this table as guest attend."[4]

Reading the motto reminds me of two occasions, separated by a decade in terms of time and by a deep ravine in terms of my response. There was the evening when I welcomed two college friends. After dinner our lively conversation turned to the political views of a third. *Over the top. Attila the Hun. Can you believe it?* Reacting to my guest's disdain, I defended the absent party even though I wasn't a fellow partisan. I soon changed the subject—to vocations and transmissions.

Years later, different guests: I wish I'd done as well. I allowed, even encouraged, dinner conversation to veer into the realm of gossip that was squelched not by me but by a guest who kindly but clearly said, "I'm not comfortable with this"—*talking about him here, talking about that now.* Though I felt mildly chastised, I didn't get defensive. We turned the topic to vacations and transitions.

I'm not going to be so bold as to embroider or inscribe Augustine's maxim and hang it on my dining room wall. But my discovering its rhyme has cemented its message in my mind.

God, at my table help me to direct conversation toward topics that edify, entertain, or enlighten and to steer clear of subjects that devastate, disparage, or demean.

making it yours

1. If you have been party to conversations that turned to unhealthy gossip sessions, were you an instigator or a bystander?

2. If a bystander, how did you respond (for instance, remain silent, change the topic, speak up more dramatically, walk away)? Talk to God about the memory and your role.

An Opportunity for Renewal

Be renewed in the spirit of your minds.
—EPHESIANS 4:23

Annually, over the Fourth of July weekend, I host a dinner for a tableful of girlfriends who don't know one another very well. Late one evening, long after dessert, Sandra threw out a question to jump-start the conversation: "So what energizes y'all?"

Camilla said reading scripture. Margaret, gardening. Jane, spending time with friends. Maybe I was tired after serving up the meal, but I couldn't name anything quite so specific.

"Entertaining seems to invigorate you," Anne suggested.

I smiled. "Now that you mention it, I'd agree—yes."

One guest looked puzzled. "But you're an *introvert*," as if the word might be a synonym for *hermit.*

My friend's "leap" surprised me. "Well, but being an introvert doesn't mean I never socialize."

Truth be told, I sometimes extend invitations as an antidote to isolation. Especially around holidays, it's easy to wallow: Surely *everyone* except me is enjoying a July barbecue. Surely *everyone* except me gathers together for Thanksgiving with extended family. Surely *everyone* except me is attending a hotshot Christmas party this weekend.

It's a woebegone outlook that can quickly spiral downward if I don't consciously take action. Setting a date. Vacuuming and shopping on behalf of others. Providing the setting for a shared meal. Boiling water for tea. Each action opens a door to the next. By the end of the gathering I'm physically tired and yet emotionally renewed.

In her autobiographical *Lit: A Memoir*, Mary Karr describes her life as being "fenced off" from others and absorbed in self-pity. One breakthrough moment comes in an AA meeting where a strapping marine comments that her simple act of making coffee for the group—someone other than herself—signifies "spiritual progress."[5]

I know that being *energized* isn't necessarily synonymous with making *spiritual progress*. But as for me at my table, I'm comfortable making the leap.

God, when my spirit needs to be renewed, help me turn to ways
and means that glorify you.

making it yours

1. Make a short list of things that energize you. Is hosting (in any of its many forms) or cooking on your list?

2. Knowing your strengths and weaknesses, think of a possible scenario that would signify "spiritual progress" to you. Ask God for grace to encourage your move in that direction, toward renewal.

My NIMBY Prayer

An argument arose among [the disciples] . . . But Jesus, knowing the reasoning of their hearts, took a child and put him by his side.
—LUKE 9:46-47

W*hat just happened?* I wondered. *And here, in my living room?* A tableful of faithful women was settling in for after-dinner conversation when a theological discussion about the Creed (how did we get on *that* subject?) erupted.

One guest said she wasn't sure about some future, climactic we-shall-rise moment. Her Christian faith maintained her in the here and now. Little resurrections every day rather than one big trumpet blast.

"Did you just say you *don't* believe in the Resurrection?" another guest challenged.

The skeptic looked at me. "Did I just throw a bomb into the room?"

"I think so," I muttered, wishing I could quietly leave my own gathering.

I only vaguely remember what happened next. No one rushed to change the topic like Jesus in Luke 9; no child captured everyone's attention. Thanks to the finesse of the other guests—not my stunned silence—the conversation settled on an even plane. It was several hours before anyone made good-night overtures and twenty-four before I regained my equilibrium.

A friend who has lived in Israel sees a cultural element to social tolerance of contention. Many Jews, she says, can verbally have at it for an evening and walk away, still comrades who will cheerfully greet each other another day. My father had this ability. "We be brothers," I can hear him say after sparring with a colleague.

As a hostess I listen for and monitor the broad spectrum of quick-tongued conversation. Witty repartee and innocent teasing can be fun. I get nervous when I hear a direct challenge. When does insightful confrontation turn to insensitive accusation or even abusive bullying?

I eventually realized that the resurrection exchange unsettled me more than anyone else in the room. In this I felt fortunate. It might have been otherwise, breaching relationships.

I want my guests to feel safe in my home. Am I responsible for every conversation here? No. But it seems reasonable to ask God to attend my NIMBY prayer: If there's stressful contention, please . . . not in my backyard; not at my table; not on my watch.

Lord, I'm uncomfortable with conflict among my guests.
Help me determine when I should just relax and let it play out, when I should
change the topic or more directly intervene. May our conversations be lively
and challenging, respectful and grounded in grace.

making it yours

1. Considering your temperament, place yourself on a spectrum that runs from "seeks out and enjoys sparring" to "avoids conflict at all cost." How can this self-knowledge inform your role as a host?

2. Read Luke 9:46-48. Reflect on Jesus' approach to his disciples' argument. His tack might require quick thinking—a request to add to your prayer list.

Treasure Old and New

Every scribe who has been trained for the kingdom of heaven
is like a master of a house, who brings out of his treasure
what is new and what is old.

—MATTHEW 13:52

thought I was familiar with all the treasures—stories and metaphors—of the Gospels. But this morning I discovered a new gem, tucked in at the end of several parables. Matthew describes an ancient aspect of hosting that seems as contemporary as my modest dinner last night.

To prepare for guests, I spread my table with a linen cloth inherited from my mother. I set six places with my collectible "forest green" dinnerware, purchased at flea markets. To add an accent, I "broke in" the quirky beaded napkin rings I'd received at Christmas.

At six I welcomed five guests from church: two female friends, Penny and her husband, and a newcomer, an older man I knew only by name.

"Your home is so cozy," Penny said over appetizers. She glanced toward a grouping of framed museum prints—old masters—and then toward an expanse of fresh greenery: hibiscus, begonias, ferns.

The meal itself? Someone complimented the rice with olives. "A new recipe?"

"The slaw, yes. But not the rice. I got the recipe from my friend Wendy. She moved away about twenty-five years ago." I interjected a memory of her farewell party. "She was so happy to be getting married and yet weeping, so sad to be leaving her old friends." Conversation continued, sometimes dwelling on earlier decades and then turning to an experience of last week. By evening's end, my circle of friends was larger, my memory bank richer, my church bond stronger.

Penny has just called, debriefing the evening. In her voice, I heard gratitude and grace. I like to think the kingdom of God in my neighborhood is broader today than yesterday—for my having opened my home, drawing in and setting out the new alongside the old.

Lord, you enhance my life and ministry with old and new treasures.
Thank you.

making it yours

1. Categorize a few items in your home or recipes in your repertoire as "old treasures" and "new treasures." Do you value one type of treasure over the other? Are you satisfied with the mix? If your "old" doesn't feel like treasure, look for easy ways to spruce things up (for example, a new table runner, pillow, or lamp shade).

2. Reflect on Jesus' spiritual message in Matthew 13:52.

Wendy's Rice with Olives and Chiles

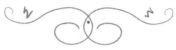

1 cup long-grain rice	1 cup grated cheddar cheese
1 cup sour cream	½ cup sliced black olives
1 (4-oz.) can chopped green chiles	

Cook the rice, making about 3 cups.

Preheat the oven to 350°F. Combine sour cream and chiles. Lightly grease a 1½-quart casserole. In the bottom place half of the hot rice, then layer the sour cream and chiles, half the cheese, half the olives. Top with the remaining rice, then cheese and olives. Bake 20 minutes.

For the full effect: I note that Wendy's original recipe called for an additional cup of Monterey Jack cheese and a full cup of olives. This scaled-back version works just fine. Serves 6.

Show and Tell?

Thou wilt shew me the path of life: in thy presence is fulness of joy.
—**PSALM 16:11,** KJV

Let us come before [the LORD'S] presence with thanksgiving.
—**PSALM 95:2,** KJV

More than twenty years ago, as my sister's houseguest I happened upon a social gathering titled "Rings and Things." "Bring some item you value because it reminds you of the days when . . . or the person who . . . Tell us the story." I still remember a few of the mementos, from the grand (a ruby ring) to the pedestrian (a hunter's lucky cap).

It worked so well, I borrowed the idea. "Bring a precious possession," I told guests, explaining my intents. If there were groans, I didn't hear them. People showed up, compliantly carrying little somethings. After dinner we told our tales. A man explained his photo of a steering wheel—the memory of his beloved vintage car. A woman who had just learned how to swim, taught by a child, pulled out her scrunched-up bathing suit. Hoping for a laugh, I displayed my father's engagement gift to my mom: bronze-plated bookends replicating a Western sculpture titled the *End of the Trail.* (Go figure.)

I tried this approach successfully on several occasions, but eventually the idea aged out. For large groups I still occasionally initiate whole-room after-dinner conversations (anecdotes and ethical ramifications of "finders, keepers"; restrictions or lessons, begrudged in youth but now appreciated), but I've set aside the request for premeditation and props. *Just come.* No pressure to perform.

In my prayer time it's easy to slip into a mode of spiritual show-and-tell, as if I'm displaying my precious possessions and telling God their representational stories, some poignant, some fortuitous, some baffling. The format works; I can see it modeled in so many of the Psalms. But the older I get, the more I'm happy to *just come.* Into God's presence. No agenda. No reports. Just come.

God, whether I'm rehashing the stories of my life or sitting quietly in your presence, you are attentive to my attentions. Thank you.

making it yours

1. If you were to bring a "precious possession" to a "show-and-tell" social function, what would you bring? What story would you tell?

2. Do you resonate with the show-and-tell model of prayer? What would an "in your presence" model look like to you?

The Honor of Your Presence

She has done a beautiful thing to me.
—MARK 14:6

We discover our gifts in the eyes of the receiver.
—HENRI J. M. NOUWEN

In the weeks before Thanksgiving, I'd invited potential guests—two couples and three singles. "Thank you very much, but . . ." It seemed they all had places to go, turkeys to eat. I might have asked others, driven across three states to be with family, or finagled an invitation, but I didn't. If someone asked of my plans, I smiled. "Just a low-key day, and you?" No specific invitations were proffered, and our conversations ended kindly.

It was a quiet week. On Sunday I made pies and cranberry relish. On Tuesday I bought some turkey legs, which I intended to bake, smothered with stuffing. On Wednesday I drove a Latina neighbor to an ethnic grocer for its poultry special.

Then Thursday morning the woman's nine-year-old daughter with special challenges sat at my table snapping dried bread crusts "the size of a quarter," I instructed. There's never anything complicated about our cross-cultural conversation. "Why is the bread so hard?" she asked. Then, "Who's coming to eat? Are you going out? My mom's cooking those three chickens she bought." Hearing intimations of no firm plans, she finally said, "You can come and eat chicken with my family, Miss Evelyn. How do you feel about that?"

"We'll see." I knew this child well enough to discount her impulsive suggestions. Her mother wasn't always on board. But at 12:30 my young neighbor yelled through the front-door mail slot: "The chicken sandwiches are ready. Are you coming?" Sandwiches. Not what I was expecting, but I said yes to a well-appointed, informally served sub. All I could eat. I patted my stomach; thank you very much. I went home and brought back half a pie. "For you, later."

"Are you coming back tonight for chicken and rice?" What? Well, there were two more chickens in the oven. "If your mom wants. Ask me again when it's ready."

In the kitchen at 5:30—my turkey legs cooked but not tasted—I heard the familiar demanding voice: "Miss Evelyn, come. It's time for chicken and rice." *Do I want to do this? What about my turkey and stuffing?* I didn't have time to dwell on the answer. The child's persistence beckoned me beyond myself.

That evening we neighbors ate El Salvadoran chicken and rice from disposable plates. "Do you want a knife? Water or soda? A napkin?"

"How do you say *thanksgiving* in Spanish?" I asked, to encourage conversation. And "What are we thankful for?" Our families and neighbors. God. "This roast chicken," I said, as my young friend reached over my plastic fork to swipe a bite of my dark meat.

"Do you like it?" she asked. "Do you want some more?" She looked straight into my eyes. In her beaming face I recognized the healthy pride of a budding hostess. She made no attempt to hide her true feelings. "Do you like my family's Thanksgiving?"

Twenty years ago I was welcomed as a guest in a home for a Thanksgiving dinner served by hired help. I attest, this was no apocryphal story: there really was a backup turkey roasted and ready to serve. It was a grand feast. And yet the memory of sitting at that polished table—china, silver, and linen—doesn't compare with the honor of being welcomed by this special child. Like Jesus describing a woman who had brazenly shown up to anoint his feet, I commend her hospitable spirit: "She has done what she could" (Mark 14:8).

God, remind me of the honor inherent in hospitality—as a hostess or guest.

making it yours

1. Reflect on a time when you realized after the fact that a host or hostess had honored you as a guest. How does that experience influence the way you welcome others?

2. Consider ways you can incorporate children into your circle of hospitality.

---

served at my table

Fresh Cranberry Relish

This is great as a holiday side dish and more: as a topping on ice cream; as breakfast fruit on cereal; as a colorful dressing on a fruit salad, such as apples, bananas, and walnuts.

1 (12-oz.) package fresh cranberries
1 orange
1 cup sugar

Wash the fruits. Cut unpeeled orange into 12 wedges. In an old-fashioned manual food grinder or a food processor, grind the cranberries and the whole orange. Add the sugar and stir. Makes about 2 cups.

A Guest's Gift

I will show you a still more excellent way.
—1 CORINTHIANS 12:31

I Came to buy a smile—today.
—EMILY DICKINSON

In an upstairs window, I've hung a hostess gift, which was transformed from a trinket to a memento by a table conversation. The bright pink crane peeks down on the well-trafficked sidewalk of my multiethnic neighborhood. But that's only the end of the story; it begins decades ago, when my older brother broke his glasses while visiting me. At the optician's I silently watched as he winsomely explained his problem, clarified his time constraints, and expressed his gratitude. I complimented him: "Wow. You did that with such finesse. I'm not very good with merchants." On our way home, he accompanied me into a different store. My encounter was quick. My manner clipped. Walking out, my brother quipped, "Well, I can see what you mean." That day something shifted. I tried an experiment. Standing at a counter—the mechanic, the bank, the post office—I smiled. The positive response surprised me, even when the person spoke a different language. A wave of recognition. A neighborly nod.

It seems so elementary, but I hardly understood what I was doing, until this spring, when a dinner guest gave me the pink bird. It looks like it's made of paper, folded in the style of Japanese origami. But actually it's a hand-crafted ceramic piece from a museum shop, wings spread to a three-inch span. She also brought eight smaller cranes, to set by each guest's plate.

The birds triggered a happy memory for John, recently widowed. He and his wife had traveled extensively overseas. When she sat near a child on a train, she reached into her purse where she kept a few extra sheets of paper. "She'd fold it into cranes, like these." He pointed to the table favors. "Children, and the parents too, were so fascinated." Seeing a bird emerge, poised for flight—"it broke through all language barriers," John said.

Ah, like a smile.

God, increase my smile. Sincerely.

making it yours

1. Has a guest given you a hostess gift that has taken on special meaning because of a conversation sparked by the gift? If possible, find the gift and dwell for a few minutes on the positive memory of the gathering and the giver. Pray for that person—for grace in his or her life and with thanksgiving.

2. When shopping, try a smile experiment. What response do you receive when you smile and treat people graciously? Is the response the same when you are more brusque?

part 5

Savoring the Taste

By the time we all said goodbye after a long and lingering dinner . . . everyone parted a little more anchored in place and friendships.
—ANDI ASHWORTH

A Peaceable Kingdom

*According to [God's] promise we are waiting for new heavens
and a new earth in which righteousness dwells. Therefore, beloved,
since you are waiting for these, be diligent to be found by him
without spot or blemish, and at peace.*
—2 PETER 3:13-14

Dishes in the sink cannot
be transformed by any act
of imagination.
—SANDRA DUGUID

I don't want to romanticize "doing" dishes, as did my father, who, though he'd never soaped a dirty cereal bowl, praised the drudging work as an opportunity for mother-daughter bonding. But I've come to see the washing of plates and cups and spoons—whether alone or companioned—as a peace of the kingdom.

My niece, a missionary just settling in to a modest house in Haiti, writes to family back home. Topic: culture shock. On the list: no dishwasher.

Hmm. I try to smile. I don't have a dishwasher. Living in vintage rentals, I never have. I occasionally, not often, wish for one, usually hours before I announce "Dinner's ready. Gather round." Long ago I realized that the best-laid meal plans call for pacing that provides an empty sink or dishwasher when guests knock on the door. I wouldn't call it clean as you go. It's more on the order of clean before they arrive. Then, at the end of the evening, I face dirty table settings, serving pieces, and a few pots, but the stacks are devoid of caked measuring cups, vegetable peelers, and mixing bowls.

"May I help you with the dishes?" someone asks, reaching for her purse, before asking for her coat.

I always say no. Anticipating a smile, I sometimes add, "You don't help with my cleanup. And when I come to your place, I won't help with yours." Over the years I've allowed a select few—with just the right familial temperament—to ignore me and draw hot water.

Discussing what she calls the quotidian mysteries, Kathleen Norris notes that as her household's dishwasher, "I admit that I generally lose sight of the fact that God is inviting me to play," like a kindergartner splashing with cups in a basin.[1] Grown-up water play with a purpose sets aright the domestic scene. It wipes away the refuse and degradation. It guards against disease and infestation.

I never finish company dishes until the next day. The drinking glasses get a final, fresh panful of detergent water, in hope of a spotless shine. When the washing task is complete and I've stowed the dishes, silver, and glassware on their rightful shelves, I try to envision a piece of a redeemed earth, the china cabinet and silver chests filled, ready and waiting for a banquet call: Dinner's ready. Gather round.

God, I can view kitchen cleanup as a drudging task or as an opportunity to set my home aright. Give me the heart that makes the peaceful choice, and may that choice reflect my ordered heart.

making it yours

1. How do you feel about cleanup after a meal? If it's a dreaded task, how do you respond to Kathleen Norris's challenge that washing dishes is an opportunity to play in and with water?

2. How can cleanup enable you to bring the peace of the kingdom to your home?

The Letdown

[God's] voice was like the roar of rushing waters.
—EZEKIEL 43:2, NIV

L ast night five friends gathered around my table. I served up a simple meal—potato salad and saucy chicken—that prompted compliments: "This is *good.*" I asked a leading question about career paths, and the conversation took off. Over dessert—my mother's special pear upside-down gingerbread—the storytelling turned to laughter and finally to someone gently acknowledging God's presence among us. Guests lingered until well past eleven. After church this morning one of them summarized the evening's success: "If that had been my party, I'd be feeling—*yes!*"

But by early afternoon, my spirits had dipped. "The letdown," my mother called it. My friends felt far away, my apartment quiet, my world small. Praying for a brighter perspective, I headed out. To where? I wasn't quite sure. To the buttressed cathedral? To the public park? I felt drawn toward a chapel courtyard, to sit beside its centerpiece fountain with twin jets shooting as high as eight feet.

At first I just watched the fountain: the fluid dance of its forceful sprays, the brief high-step jet fluctuating to more subdued splashes. In the water's rhythm I could see my hours and my days: flashes of success followed by downtimes. I could hear that both the high points and the letdowns are complementarily, equally, full of grace. "I'm hearing God in the fountain," I wrote in my journal. Refreshed by a new awareness of God's presence, I was ready to return home, even anticipating a light supper of leftover salad and cake turned upside down.

Lord, grace me with reminders of your presence.

making it yours

1. When the "letdown" hits, what can you do or where can you go to refresh your spirits?

2. Work with the fountain metaphor to grasp the reality of the ebb and flow of your emotional life.

Mom's Pear Upside-Down Gingerbread*

For the fruit bottom:
¼ cup melted butter or margarine
⅓ cup honey or brown sugar
7 pear halves, fresh or canned (If
  using fresh pears, heat the pears
  in the butter mixture in the oven as
  you prepare the cake.)

For the gingerbread:
5 tablespoons light brown sugar
1 egg
¼ cup oil
½ cup sour milk (milk plus ½ tablespoon vinegar)
¼ cup molasses
1 cup flour
½ teaspoon baking soda
2 teaspoons cinnamon
1 teaspoon ginger
¼ teaspoon nutmeg

Preheat the oven to 350°F. Cover the bottom of a 9-inch round (or 9 x 9 square) cake pan with the melted butter blended with the honey. Place the pear halves flat side down on the butter mixture. If using a round pan, place the pear halves in a circle, narrow ends pointing toward the center of the pan.

With an electric beater, mix the sugar, egg, and wet ingredients. Add the dry ingredients and mix until smooth. Pour the gingerbread cake batter over the pears. Bake for 40 minutes. Serve warm or cold as an upside-down cake (pears on top) with vanilla ice cream, whipped cream, or in a small bowl of milk.

The cake can also be made using a commercial gingerbread mix. But Mom's is milder.

*Adapted from America's Cookbook (New York: Scribner, 1937), probably a wedding gift to my mother.

God, have mercy on me, a sinner.
—LUKE 18:13, NIV

When setting up an informal supper, my guests and I had agreed on a few basics. Driving from a distance to get here, Carol and Mary had proposed a four o'clock arrival. But once on the road, they'd call and confirm, depending on traffic and who knew what else. "What can we bring?" they'd asked.

"Just a beverage," I said. "I'll take care of the food."

So last evening, about four, I set the table though Carol and Mary hadn't called. Nor by five. About 5:30 I put the table-ready casserole in a warm oven. At six I paced. At 6:30 I called a friend to vent. *Jeepers.* At 6:45 the phone rang: "Hey, there. We're near you but lost—and have been for an hour." By seven, three hours late, two of which were never explained, they knocked at my door, frustrated (no more than I), happy to see me, hungry. And—what?—empty handed. (Wait—hadn't this happened the last time they came?)

Why hadn't they called earlier? They had excuses. They'd tried my disconnected cell phone. My landline number was buried in a suitcase in their car trunk. They were hoping I'd call Mary's cell phone. Sigh.

At table, they seemed to enjoy the thick soup and overcooked casserole. We caught up on one another's lives. As they left, they offhandedly thanked me for my patience. But I sensed they were hardly aware of their thoughtlessness.

At church this morning the congregation asked our "most merciful Father" to "forgive us our sins, known and unknown." As I quickly examined my week—did I snub a neighbor? neglect a commitment?—I also remembered my guests' shortcomings. I silently opened my hands and accepted the possibility that they and I are one. I prayed:

Lord, have mercy on us all.

making it yours

1. If something like this had happened to you, how would you have responded? (Or maybe it has! How did you respond?)

2. It's so much easier to see others' shortcomings than to see our own. How does "Lord, have mercy" apply to you today?

Risk Analysis

Cast your bread upon the waters, for you will find it after many days.
—ECCLESIASTES 11:1

Accommodating my dad in his pastoral role, my mom was an inveterate hostess, logging, for tax purposes, up to six hundred servings a year. Down-home cooking, rarely more venturesome than mustard and Worcestershire. But guests appreciated her efforts—mostly.

One weekend, hosting strangers interviewing for a church job, she laid out a roast turkey dinner with mashed potatoes, bread stuffing, and gravy. Standard company fare. Right fine in my view, then a high school senior. But as Mom washed the dishes, she succinctly summarized the dinner: "That didn't work."

"What do you mean?"

"They didn't like it. They didn't appreciate it. It was a flop."

My affirmations didn't penetrate her negative assessment.

Several years later she again felt disrespected, when only one couple came to a New Year's open house—an afternoon buffet set out for fifty.

It's easier to write about my mother's failures than my own. The New Year's Eve party for twenty-something peers who claimed they didn't like parties. (Did I fall asleep watching TV at my own do?) The invitations refused, some by way of Miss Manners's practiced approach, "You are so kind, but . . . " and some less adroitly. The no-shows or apologies that someone forgot. The meals or desserts that I've chosen to forget or rosily gloss.

Entertaining—extending an invitation, say nothing of opening the door to an unbidden neighbor—is a risk. Every time. Even if hospitality is perceived to be one's spiritual gift.

An unexpected biblical find—buried under the cast-your-bread-upon-the-waters topic sentence of Ecclesiastes 11—helps to refocus my vision: "In the morning sow your seed, and at evening withhold not your hand, for you do not know which will prosper, this or that, or whether both alike will be good" (v. 6). Be generous, the wisdom writer says, but understand the realities: Some efforts "prosper" and some don't. Sometimes the food and the conversation "work"; sometimes neither. Sometimes we feel affirmed; sometimes we don't. Sometimes the bread cast upon the waters becomes a free-floating memory for God to redeem further down the river of time.

God, disappointment with the results of one risk can so easily keep us from venturing another. Give us courage braced with wisdom as we reach out beyond ourselves and offer sustenance for table guests.

making it yours

1. Do you have painful memories of gatherings you hosted that "flopped," as my mother would have said? How did you respond at the time? How did things settle out eventually? In a different context, have you tried or can you try to reach out again?

2. Every aspect of hosting requires courage, which often comes as we turn to God for strength. Write a prayer, asking for grace and its attendant courage.

Thank You, Thank You

[The leper] fell on his face at Jesus' feet, giving him thanks . . . Then Jesus answered, "Were not ten cleansed? Where are the nine? Was no one found to return and give praise to God except this foreigner?"
—LUKE 17:16-18

Now and again, when sorting piles of papers or photos, I'll come across an old thank-you note, squirreled away. I'll glance at a few lines and immediately see why the note never made its way into the trash bin: a guest has seemingly sincerely effused appreciation.

I'm suddenly sorry that one of the most memorable notes went to the recycle container last week, something about a conversational "salon." I've scrounged and found a few others: ". . . one of the highlights of our spring/summer" (alongside the birth of first grandchildren). And "How is it that women—some of whom see each other only around your table—can jump into conversation and swim in the deep-end of thought and being?"

Of course some thank-yous come by phone, a welcomed opportunity for a quick debriefing. Some by e-mail, the best being more than 140 characters. But so many, never received, have flown forgotten in a dream world of good intention. I tread lightly here, as I myself have been remiss in expressing gratitude. Like nine of the ten happily healed of leprosy, I've been guilty of too quickly running off to the new day without giving thanks.

On the other hand, as a hostess I've occasionally acted on urges to pick up the phone and thank guests for an insightful comment or thoughtful gesture—realizing that the time together "worked" because of a grace they provided, not I. I think of this as I reread the first line of one of these newly discovered thank-you notes, from Jennifer: "What a wonderful evening you showed us." I'm surprised by the verb—*showed*—as if I had enabled a small group to see something already in their midst.

Jesus said, "Where two or three are gathered in my name, there am I among them" (Matt. 18:20). Sitting at the table. For this I say,

Lord, thank you, thank you.

making it yours

1. Have you ever wanted to thank a guest for a special contribution to a gathering—whether it was a tasty food item, a discussion point, or a thoughtful action? Think of doing so in the future.

2. Express thanks to a person and to God for some kindness or grace—today.

What's This?

When the people of Israel saw it, they said to one another, "What is it?"
For they did not know what it was. And Moses said to them, "It is the
bread that the LORD has given you to eat."

—EXODUS 16:15

One April I froze a little blossom, snipped from my yard, in each ice cube I later slipped into water glasses as Sunday guests arrived. At dinner my Ukrainian friend, Tatiana, took a sip and then smiled quizzically. "What's this—purple?"

"A violet," I said.

English is Tatiana's third language, which might explain why she didn't remember the name of the delicate edible flower that soon floated to the bottom of her tumbler. And months later, when she tried to replicate my frozen garnish, I was the one who smiled quizzically. "I went to a florist," she reported, "and asked to buy those tiny flowers. They just didn't understand what I was looking for."

"A florist wouldn't have violets," I gently explained. "They're wild-flowers; some people say weeds. I'll give you some." So the next spring I dug up a few of the shiny-leafed plants and sent them to Tatiana, clear across the city. A few days later she called to say thank you and also to disclose her find: "I didn't know: I already have this flower in my own yard."

This morning I awoke convinced that I'm lacking some God-given je ne sais quoi—a natural talent or beauty or mystique—that would be the perfect complement to my workaday, plod-along life. This afternoon, when I plunked a few ice cubes into a glass of tea—made from mint snipped from my yard—the Spirit reminded me of Tatiana and the delight of her unexpected discovery.

Lord, you have given me all I need to live an abundant life. Help me to find any unidentified resources that are right under my nose.

making it yours

1. Try to identify an area of your life in which you feel a lack but for which a resource might already be close at hand.

2. Write a prayer, reflecting on Tatiana's discovery, including thanks and a request for new discoveries.

For the Pleasure

Looking to Jesus, the founder and perfecter of our faith,
who for the joy that was set before him endured the cross.
—HEBREWS 12:2

served guests a labor-intensive meal, including three vegetable salads and peach crisp. After dinner, my friend Patricia said, "This was a lot of work—thank you."

"It's my pleasure," I responded. I don't use the phrase often enough, but when I do, I mean it. To me it's not a mindless cliché, tacked on to a thank-you ritual. It names the satisfaction I feel in honoring others.

It's all because of a child—I don't know her name—I met years ago. Her dad was a friend of my dad's, after I'd grown up and moved away to "the city." Well, mostly "grown up"; I admit that I still expected my dad to change the oil in my car when I visited on holiday weekends. One busy Saturday Dad asked this friend to do the dirty work. Mr. Friend came over, bringing along his elementary-school–age daughter, who played nearby as her dad drained the pan, changed the filter, and added new 10W-30.

As Mr. Friend finally wiped his hands clean, I thanked him profusely. "Oh, you're quite welcome," he said. I pulled a bill from my pocket and tried to pay him. "Oh, no," he responded, refusing the cash. "Please," I pleaded.

That's when his daughter spoke up: "He did it for the pleasure." I hardly understood her meaning, until her dad interpreted: "She's right. It's *my* pleasure."

That girl is grown up by now. Wherever she is, I thank her for twisting a tired idiom into a memorable motive. My next dinner party? A lot of work, as always. But serving my guests? I intend to do it for the pleasure.

Jesus, with joy and for joy, you served others.
Help me to follow your example.

making it yours

1. For you is "It's my pleasure" a cliché or a meaningful response?

2. Though it may be hard to get your head around Hebrews 12:2, try to work with it. Journal a few paragraphs about "the joy that was set before" Jesus—and, in a different context and setting, the joy set before you.

Swedish Apple Pie

After I'd left home, my mom got this recipe from a fellow parsonage host-ess, Kris Jack. It is so easy and good, served with ice cream, that my dad eventually complained that he was tired of it—that it was the only dessert she ever served to company.

Preheat the oven to 350°F.

Mix well with a fork or spoon:

1 egg
¾ cup sugar
½ cup flour
1 teaspoon baking powder
1 teaspoon vanilla

½ teaspoon salt
1 apple, peeled, cored, and chopped
  to the size of raisins (about 1 cup)
⅓ cup chopped walnuts or pecans
  (optional)

Place in a greased 9-inch pie pan. Top with cinnamon sugar: 2 tablespoons sugar combined with ½ teaspoon cinnamon.

Bake 30 minutes. Serve warm or cool with vanilla, maple walnut, or butter pecan ice cream or whipped cream.

A Medium Day?

Who has despised the day of small things?
—ZECHARIAH 4:10, NKJV

A young neighbor girl and I have settled in to an after-school greeting: "Hi, there. How was your day?" Our answers range from "good" (thumbs up) to "bad" (thumbs down), with an intermediate "medium" (hand flutter).

Last evening she shifted the ritual into a future tense: "Miss Evelyn, tomorrow, will you have a good day? Or bad day? Or . . . ?" She made a seesaw with her fingers.

I overexplain the nature of the future. Not expecting any significant highs or lows, I summarize, "I hope I'll have a medium or good day, and I pray for one, but I can't really know."

That conversation reminds me of another that I overheard from the backseat of a car, riding to a restaurant for a final meal before neighbors moved away to an overseas assignment. Whenever we went out—a pancake house, a sit-down hamburger chain, an all-you-can-eat buffet—they picked up the check. This time, as sometimes previous, I was fussing that I would pay my way. I would even treat their farewell.

Passenger Marti turned to her husband, in the driver's seat. "No," she said emphatically, as if I weren't listening. "When you were away at school . . . one night I had no money. I was exhausted and strung out. I knocked on Evelyn's door and asked her for food. She gave me dinner. When we go out to eat, she doesn't pay."

Did I hear correctly? Yes, Marti had sometimes knocked on my door when she got home late from work. Yes, I'd invited her in. And found her some refrigerated leftovers a few times as our friendship grew. But I didn't see any evening's request as frantic or any particular meal as pivotal. To me they were all just part of a rather medium day, neither wonderful nor disastrous, a day of small things.

Maybe that's what the lunch-packing Galilean mother was anticipating when she sent her son off to hear Jesus, the itinerant teacher come to town. "I'll give you a few extra rolls in case you get caught in the traffic or run into one of your school buddies." She wasn't expecting to hear a late-night report of her fillet sandwiches, pulled from a backpack, multiplied to feed a hillside seating of five thousand, with miraculous fragments brought back home.

You never know what God can do with tomorrow—even if it's a medium day.

> Such a day of small things still, but on God's terms, and that is enough. Size as well as time and space count nothing with Him.[2]

Lord, I give you this ho-hum day, this average week, not knowing what you might make of it. Lead me along some path that provides opportunity for us, you and me, to restore someone's body or spirit.

making it yours

1. Think of a time when you reached out to someone in what you thought was a ho-hum way, representing a medium day—but then you later realized you'd delivered more grace than you'd expected.

2. Write a note of encouragement to yourself, including gratitude for God's ability to use you in ways you couldn't previously imagine.

Feed My Lambs

Thou preparest a table before me.
—PSALM 23:5, KJV

L ast evening I returned home from spending twenty-four hours with my friend John, prematurely ravaged by Alzheimer's. At dinner, breakfast, and lunch I offered to spell his aides: patiently, heartbreakingly spoon-feeding him as if he were a drooling, teething child. "We're accustomed to feeding our babies and our elderly parents," my sister tells me, "but not our peers. It's a whole nother level" of caretaking, service, hospitality.

After two of three meals, while John slept, I pulled a book from his shelf and read a wartime story that quoted an old gospel song usually associated with evangelism—saving souls from the shoals. But in the context of my day's ministrations—at the next meal I'd coax John even to open his mouth—the merciful metaphor expanded its challenge, seeming to overlay my efforts with grace:

Brightly beams our Father's mercy
    From his lighthouse evermore;
But to us he gives the keeping
    Of the lights along the shore.[3]

Strung out at church this morning—Good Shepherd Sunday—I didn't really notice much more than the broad strokes of one line of Psalm 23: someone was preparing a table for someone else. But who and whom? It seemed a little vague.

Midway through the service, as an usher I carried the Communion bread up the aisle to the altar. *Receive and bless, this, our offering, Lord.* Minutes later, at God's Table, I swallowed a hallowed meal. Christ, our Passover, sacrificed for us. Let us keep the feast.

John 21 shows a merciful Jesus standing along a shoreline, cooking and serving his disciples a breakfast. "Come and dine," he says. In the same scene he passes the torch to his followers, commissioning Peter to feed his sheep, even the most vulnerable lambs.

Who's preparing a table for whom? I'm still puzzling out the answer.

"Gentle Shepherd, come and feed us,"[4] *so that we in turn*
have strength to nourish others.

making it yours

1. What does Jesus' request to "feed my sheep" mean for you?

2. Consider the wide range of your hosting efforts. In reading this book, how have you come to a broader understanding of God's offer to prepare a table before you?

Epigraph Sources and Notes

Introduction

Epigraph

Eugene H. Peterson, *Christ Plays in Ten Thousand Places: A Conversation in Spiritual Theology* (Grand Rapids, MI: Eerdmans, 2005), 212.

Prelude: Water with Ice, Please

Epigraph

Margaret Feinberg, *Hungry for God: Hearing God's Voice in the Ordinary and the Everyday* (Grand Rapids, MI: Zondervan, 2011), 43.

Part 1: Setting the Scene

Epigraphs

Karen Burton Mains, *Open Heart, Open Home: The Hospitable Way to Make Others Feel Welcome and Wanted* (Downers Grove, IL: InterVarsity Press, 2002), 23.

Margaret Kim Peterson, *Keeping House: The Litany of Everyday Life* (San Francisco: Jossey-Bass, 2007), 17.

The Compact Catholic Prayer Book, compiled by the editors of Word Among Us Press (Frederick, MD: Word Among Us Press, 2008), 17.

1. Bonnie Thurston, "Guess Who Ought to Be Coming to Dinner," *Cathedral Age* (Winter 2004): 22.
2. Paul Tournier, *The Meaning of Gifts* (Atlanta: John Knox Press, 1963), 28, quoted in Tournier, *Reflections on Life's Most Crucial Questions* (New York: Harper and Row, 1976), 60.
3. Marcia Brown, *Stone Soup* (New York: Scribner, 1947).

4. Robert Farrar Capon, *The Supper of the Lamb: A Culinary Reflection* (1969; repr., New York: Simon and Schuster, Pocket Books, 1970), 162.

Part 2: Stirring the Pot

Epigraphs
Michael Pollan, interviewed in Ruth Reichl, "The American Table," *Smithsonian* (June 2013): 81.
Phyllis Pellman Good and Rachel Thomas Pellman, *From Amish and Mennonite Kitchens* (Intercourse, PA: Good Books, 1984), 7.
Molly O'Neill, *The Pleasure of Your Company: How to Give a Dinner Party without Losing Your Mind* (New York: Viking, 1997), 16.
Vinita Hampton Wright, *Velma Still Cooks in Leeway* (Nashville, TN: Broadman and Holman, 2000), 23.
Charles Wesley, "O Thou Who Camest from Above," *The United Methodist Hymnal* (Nashville, TN: United Methodist Publishing House, 1990), 501.
J. Brent Bill and Beth A. Booram, *Awaken Your Senses: Exercises for Exploring the Wonder of God* (Downers Grove, IL: InterVarsity Press, 2012), 26.

1. Edwin Holt Hughes, "Thanksgiving for Life's Variety," *Thanksgiving Sermons*, Christian Festival Series (Cincinnati, OH: Jennings and Graham, 1909), 45.
2. What about copyright? you ask. Lists, say, of ingredients, can't be copyrighted, though recipe instructions are another story.
3. Miriam Huffman Rockness, ed., *A Blossom in the Desert: Reflections of Faith in the Art and Writings of Lilias Trotter* (Grand Rapids, MI: Discovery House, 2007), 115. Originally from Trotter's journal, August 8, 1899.
4. Mary K. Mohler, "Biblical Hospitality," in *The Christian Homemaker's Handbook*, ed. Pat Ennis and Dorothy Kelley Patterson (Wheaton, IL: Crossway, 2013), 389.
5. Miriam Huffman Rockness, *Home, God's Design: Celebrating a Sense of Place* (Grand Rapids, MI: Zondervan, 1990), 179, noting a hospitality principle of Edith Schaeffer.
6. Nelson Mandela, "Inaugural Speech, Pretoria [Mandela] 5/10/94," African Studies Center, University of Pennsylvania, accessed March 4, 2014, http://www.africa.upenn.edu/Articles_Gen/Inaugural_Speech_17984.html.

Part 3: Serving Up Soup

Epigraphs
Margaret Kim Peterson, *Keeping House: The Litany of Everyday Life* (San Francisco: Jossey-Bass, 2007), 128.

Eugenia Price, *Woman to Woman* (Grand Rapids, MI: Zondervan, 1959), 116. Italics in original.

Margaret Feinberg, *Hungry for God: Hearing God's Voice in the Ordinary and the Everyday* (Grand Rapids, MI: Zondervan, 2011), 54.

1. James Thurber, *Further Fables for Our Time* (New York: Simon and Schuster, 1956), 152.
2. F. A. Graves, "Honey in the Rock" (1895), http://www.hymnary.org/text /o_my_brother_do_you_know_the_savior_who._
3. John Ruskin, *Modern Painters*, vol. 5, *Of General Principles and of Truth* (Boston, MA: Dana Estes, 1887), 405.
4. From the *Tanakh: A New Translation of the Holy Scriptures according to the Traditional Hebrew Text* (Philadelphia, PA: Jewish Publication Society, 1985).
5. Dorothy Day, *The Long Loneliness: The Autobiography of the Legendary Catholic Social Activist* (1952; repr., San Francisco: HarperOne, 2009), 285.

Part 4: Sitting at Table
Epigraphs
Henri J. M. Nouwen, "A Place of Vulnerability and Trust," in *Bread for the Journey: A Daybook of Wisdom and Faith* (San Francisco: HarperSanFrancisco, 1997), reading for October 3.
Henri J. M. Nouwen, *Reaching Out: The Three Movements of the Spiritual Life* (1975; repr., New York: Image Books, 1986), 87.
Emily Dickinson, "I Came to buy a smile—today—," *The Complete Poems of Emily Dickinson,* ed. Thomas H. Johnson (Boston, MA: Little, Brown, 1960), 102.

1. John Cennick, "Be Present at Our Table, Lord," *The United Methodist Hymnal* (Nashville, TN: United Methodist Publishing House, 1990), 621.
2. Suzanne von Drachenfels, "The Art of Tables and Table Manners," accessed November 1, 2013, www.tabletalk.org/tipsonmanners.htm.
3. See Judith Martin, "Miss Manners," *Washington Post*, May 29, 2013: "Instant research has a discouraging effect on conversation."
4. Cited in "Israel Museum Unveils Largest Excavated Painting," *Biblical Archaeology Review* (September–October 2010): 17.
5. Mary Karr, *Lit: A Memoir* (New York: HarperCollins, 2009), 206.

Part 5: Savoring the Taste

Epigraphs

Andi Ashworth, "Taking the Long View in a Life of Hospitality," *Art House America* blog post, October 17, 2013, http://www.arthouseamerica.com/blog/taking-the-long-view-in-a-life-of-hospitality.html, originally published by Ransom Fellowship, www.ransomfellowship.org.

Sandra Duguid, "Dishes in the Sink," in *Pails Scrubbed Silver* (St. Cloud, MN: North Star Press, 2013), 75.

1. Kathleen Norris, *The Quotidian Mysteries: Laundry, Liturgy and "Women's Work"* (Mahwah, NJ: Paulist Press, 1998), 27.
2. Miriam Huffman Rockness, ed., *A Blossom in the Desert: Reflections of Faith in the Art and Writings of Lilias Trotter* (Grand Rapids, MI: Discovery House, 2007), 203. Originally from Trotter's journal, January 1, 1902.
3. Philip P. Bliss, "Let the Lower Lights Be Burning" (1871), quoted in Homer Hickam, "Dosie, of Killakeet Island," in Bret Lott, ed., *The Best Christian Short Stories* (Nashville, TN: Thomas Nelson, 2006), 141.
4. "Gentle Shepherd," song lyric by Gloria Gaither (1974), quoted in Gloria Gaither, *Because He Lives: The Stories and Inspiration Behind the Songs of Bill and Gloria Gaither* (Grand Rapids, MI: Zondervan, 1997), 112.

About the Author

Evelyn Bence is known for her warm, personal writing style. She is the author of *Prayers for Girlfriends and Sisters and Me*, *Spiritual Moments with the Great Hymns*, and *Mary's Journal*, an award-winning novel written in the voice of Jesus' mother. She's coauthor of *Just as We Were: A Nostalgic Look at Growing Up Born Again* and compiler of numerous inspirational collections.

Evelyn's personal essays have appeared in publications including *The Washington Post*, *Books & Culture*, *Christianity Today*, and *US Catholic*. She is an ongoing contributor to the *Daily Guideposts* annual devotional.

Evelyn lives in Arlington, Virginia. She has served as religion editor at Doubleday, managing editor for *Today's Christian Woman* magazine, and senior editor at Prison Fellowship Ministries. She is a graduate of Houghton College.

CPSIA information can be obtained at www.ICGtesting.com
Printed in the USA
LVOW04s2311290914

406434LV00005B/5/P